THE PELICAN SHAKESPEARE
GENERAL EDITOR : ALFRED HARBAGE
AB II
TWELFTH NIGHT

WILLIAM SHAKESPEARE

Twelfth Night, or, What You Will

EDITED BY

CHARLES T. PROUTY

PENGUIN BOOKS

BALTIMORE · MARYLAND

This edition first published 1958
Reprinted 1960, 1963, 1965, 1966 (twice)
Penguin Books Inc.
3300 Clipper Mill Road, Baltimore, Maryland 21211

Library of Congress Catalog Card
Number 57–8514

Printed in the United States of America

CONTENTS

Shakespeare and His Stage   7

The Texts of the Plays   12

Introduction   15

Twelfth Night, or, What You Will   29

SHAKESPEARE AND HIS STAGE

William Shakespeare was christened in Holy Trinity Church, Stratford-on-Avon, April 26, 1564. His birth is traditionally assigned to April 23rd. He was the eldest of four boys and two girls who survived infancy in the family of John Shakespeare, glover and trader of Henley Street, and his wife Mary Arden, daughter of a small landowner of Wilmcote. In 1568 John was elected Bailiff (equivalent to Mayor) of Stratford, having already filled the minor municipal offices. The town maintained for the sons of the burgesses a free school, taught by a university graduate and offering preparation in Latin sufficient for university entrance; its early registers are lost, but there can be little doubt that Shakespeare received the formal part of his education in this school.

On November 27, 1582, a license was issued for the marriage of William Shakespeare (aged eighteen) and Ann Hathaway (aged twenty-six), and on May 26, 1583, their child Susanna was christened in Holy Trinity Church. The inference that the marriage was forced upon the youth is natural but not inevitable; betrothal was legally binding at the time, and was sometimes regarded as conferring conjugal rights. Two additional children of the marriage, the twins Hamnet and Judith, were christened on February 2, 1585. Meanwhile the prosperity of the elder Shakespeares had declined, and William was impelled to seek a career outside Stratford.

The tradition that he spent some time as a country teacher is old but unverifiable. Because of the absence of records his early twenties are called the "lost years," and only one thing about them is certain – that at least some of these years were spent in winning a place in the acting profession. He may have begun as a provincial trouper, but by 1592 he was established in London and prominent enough to be attacked. In a pamphlet of that year, *Groatsworth of Wit*, the ailing Robert Greene complained of the neglect which university writers like himself had suffered from actors, one of whom was daring to set up as a playwright:

> . . . an upstart crow beautified with our feathers, that with his *Tiger's heart wrapt in a player's hide* supposes he is as well able to bombast out a blank verse as the best of you, and being an absolute Johannes-factotum, is in his own conceit the only Shake-scene in a country.

The pun on his name, and the parody of his line "O tiger's heart wrapt in a woman's hide" (*3 Henry VI*), pointed clearly to Shakespeare. Some of his admirers protested, and Henry Chettle, the editor of Greene's pamphlet, saw fit to apologize:

> I am as sorry as if the original fault had been my fault, because myself have seen his demeanor no less civil than he excellent in the quality he professes. Besides divers of worship have reported his uprightness of dealing, which argues his honesty, and his facetious grace in writing that approves his art. (Prefatory epistle, *Kind Heart's Dream*)

The plague closed the London theatres for many months in 1593–94, denying the actors their livelihood. To this period belong Shakespeare's two narrative poems, *Venus and Adonis* and *Rape of Lucrece*, both dedicated to the Earl

8

of Southampton. No doubt the poet was rewarded with a gift of money as usual in such cases, but he did no further dedicating and we have no reliable information on whether Southampton, or anyone else, became his regular patron. His sonnets, first mentioned in 1598 and published without his consent in 1609, are intimate without being explicitly autobiographical. They seem to commemorate the poet's friendship with an idealized youth, rivalry with a more favored poet, and love affair with a dark mistress; and his bitterness when the mistress betrays him in conjunction with the friend; but it is difficult to decide precisely what the "story" is, impossible to decide whether it is fictional or true. The true distinction of the sonnets, at least of those not purely conventional, rests in the universality of the thoughts and moods they express, and in their poignancy and beauty.

In 1594 was formed the theatrical company known until 1603 as the Lord Chamberlain's Men, thereafter as the King's Men. Its original membership included, besides Shakespeare, the beloved clown Will Kempe and the famous actor Richard Burbage. The company acted in various London theatres and even toured the provinces, but it is chiefly associated in our minds with the Globe Theatre built on the south bank of the Thames in 1599. Shakespeare was an actor and joint owner of this company (and its Globe) through the remainder of his creative years. His plays, written at the average rate of two a year, together with Burbage's acting won it its place of leadership among the London companies.

Individual plays began to appear in print, in editions both honest and piratical, and the publishers became increasingly aware of the value of Shakespeare's name on the title pages. As early as 1598 he was hailed as the leading English dramatist in the *Palladis Tamia* of Francis Meres:

As Plautus and Seneca are accounted the best for Comedy and Tragedy among the Latins, so Shakespeare among the English is the most excellent in both kinds for the stage: for Comedy, witness his *Gentlemen of Verona*, his *Errors*, his *Love labors lost*, his *Love labors won* [at one time in print but no longer extant, at least under this title], his *Midsummers night dream*, & his *Merchant of Venice;* for Tragedy, his *Richard the 2*, *Richard the 3*, *Henry the 4*, *King John*, *Titus Andronicus*, and his *Romeo and Juliet.*

The note is valuable both in indicating Shakespeare's prestige and in helping us to establish a chronology. In the second half of his writing career, history plays gave place to the great tragedies; and farces and light comedies gave place to the problem plays and symbolic romances. In 1623, seven years after his death, his former fellow actors, John Hemming and Henry Condell, cooperated with a group of London printers in bringing out his plays in collected form. The volume is generally known as the First Folio.

Shakespeare had never severed his relations with Stratford. His wife and children may sometimes have shared his London lodgings, but their home was Stratford. His son Hamnet was buried there in 1596, and his daughters Susanna and Judith were married there in 1607 and 1616 respectively. (His father, for whom he had secured a coat of arms and thus the privilege of writing himself gentleman, died in 1601, his mother in 1608.) His considerable earnings in London, as actor-sharer, part owner of the Globe, and playwright, were invested chiefly in Stratford property. In 1597 he purchased for £60 New Place, one of the two most imposing residences in the town. A number of other business transactions, as well as minor episodes in his career, have left documentary records. By 1611 he was in a position to retire, and he seems gradually to have withdrawn from theatrical activity in order to live in Stratford. In March, 1616, he made a will, leaving token bequests to Burbage, Hemming, and Condell, but the bulk of his estate to his family. The most famous feature of the will, the bequest of the second-best bed to his wife, reveals nothing about Shakespeare's marriage; the quaintness of the provision seems commonplace to those familiar with ancient testaments. Shakespeare died April 23, 1616, and was buried in the Stratford church where he had been christened. Within seven years a monument was erected to his memory on the north wall of the chancel. Its portrait bust and the Droeshout engraving on the title page of the First Folio provide the only likenesses with an established claim to authenticity. The best verbal vignette was written by his rival Ben Jonson, the more impressive for being imbedded in a context mainly critical:

> . . . I loved the man, and do honor his memory (on this side idolatry) as much as any. He was indeed honest, and of an open and free nature: he had an excellent fancy, brave notions, and gentle expressions. . . . (*Timber or Discoveries, c.* 1623–30)

The reader of Shakespeare's plays is aided by a general knowledge of the way in which they were staged. The King's Men acquired a roofed and artificially lighted theatre only toward the close of Shakespeare's career, and then only for winter use. Nearly all his plays were designed for performance in such structures as the Globe – a three-tiered amphitheatre with a large rectangular platform extending to the center of its yard. The plays were staged by daylight, by large casts brilliantly costumed, but with only a minimum of properties, without scenery, and quite possibly without intermissions. There was a rear stage gallery for action "above," and a curtained rear recess for "discoveries" and other special effects, but by far the major portion of any play was enacted upon the projecting platform, with episode following episode in swift succession, and with shifts of time and place signaled the audience only by the momentary clearing of the stage between the episodes. Information about the identity of the characters and, when necessary, about the time and place of the action was incorporated in the dialogue. No additional indications of place have been inserted in the present editions; these are apt to obscure the original fluidity of structure, with the emphasis upon action and speech rather than scenic background. The acting, including that of the youthful apprentices to the profession who performed the parts of women, was highly skillful, with a premium placed upon grace of gesture and beauty of diction. The audiences, a cross section of the general public, commonly numbered a thousand, sometimes more than two thousand. Judged by the type of plays they applauded, these audiences were not only large but also perceptive.

THE TEXTS OF THE PLAYS

About half of Shakespeare's plays appeared in print for the first time in the folio volume of 1623. The others had been published individually, usually in quarto volumes, during his lifetime or in the six years following his death. The copy used by the printers of the quartos varied greatly in merit, sometimes representing Shakespeare's true text, sometimes only a debased version of that text. The copy used by the printers of the folio also varied in merit, but was chosen with care. Since it consisted of the best available manuscripts, or the more acceptable quartos (although frequently in editions other than the first), or of quartos corrected by reference to manuscripts, we have good or reasonably good texts of most of the thirty-seven plays.

In the present series, the plays have been newly edited from quarto or folio texts depending, when a choice offered, upon which is now regarded by bibliographical specialists as the more authoritative. The ideal has been to reproduce the chosen texts with as few alterations as possible, beyond occasional relineation, expansion of abbreviations, and modernization of punctuation and spelling. Emendation is held to a minimum, and such material as has been added, in the way of stage directions and lines supplied by an alternative text, has been enclosed in square brackets.

None of the plays printed in Shakespeare's lifetime were divided into acts and scenes, and the inference is that the author's own manuscripts were not so divided. In the folio collection, some of the plays remained undivided, some were divided into acts, and some were divided into acts and scenes. During the eighteenth century all of the plays were divided into acts and scenes, and in the Cambridge edition of the mid-nineteenth century, from which the influential Globe text derived, this division was more or less regularized and the lines were numbered. Many useful works of reference employ the act-scene-line apparatus established by the Globe text.

Since the act-scene division thus established is obviously convenient, but is of very dubious authority so far as Shakespeare's own structural principles are concerned, or the original manner of staging his plays, a problem is presented to modern editors. In the present series the act-scene division of the Globe text is retained marginally, and may be viewed as a reference aid like the line numbering. A printer's ornament marks the points of division when these points have been determined by a cleared stage indicating a shift of time and place in the action of the play, or when no harm results from the editorial assumption that there is such a shift. However, at those points where the established division is clearly misleading – that is, where continuous action has been split up into separate "scenes" – the ornament is omitted and the distortion corrected. This mechanical expedient seemed the best means of combining utility and accuracy.

The General Editor.

INTRODUCTION

On Candlemas Day, 1602, the Gentlemen of the Middle
Temple, one of the Inns of Court, held their feast, and for
their entertainment there was performed ". . . a play called
'Twelue Night, or What You Will'. . . ." John Manningham, a spectator on this occasion, continues his account
with a description of the play, which was

> . . . much like the Commedy of Errores, or Menechmi
> in Plautus, but most like and neere to that in Italian
> called *Inganni*. A good practise in it to make the Stew-
> ard beleeve his Lady widdowe was in love with him,
> by counterfeyting a letter as from his Lady in generall
> termes, telling him what shee liked best in him, and
> prescribing his gesture in smiling, his apparaile, &c.,
> and then when he came to practise making him be-
> leeue they tooke him to be mad.

Since other evidence suggests that *Twelfth Night* may
have been written as early as 1599, we may safely date it
"about 1600." Whether it was written before *As You Like
It* or *Much Ado about Nothing*, both certainly in existence by
1600, cannot be determined exactly. Actually all three of
these "Joyous Comedies" are thematically of a piece, and
any precise ordering of their composition can only be based
on subjective judgments. In some ways it is tempting to
accept Dr. Leslie Hotson's recent theory that *Twelfth Night*
was first performed on January 6, 1601, before the Queen
at Whitehall with Don Virginio Orsino as an honored
guest. There are, however, several objections to this theory

and we must still rely on the approximate date of 1600. That the visiting Italian nobleman would have been flattered by the character of the Duke Orsino is somewhat difficult to understand.

In contrast to *As You Like It*, which has a single source, the sources or analogues of *Twelfth Night* are manifold. Manningham refers to two possible sources, Plautus's *Menaechmi* and the Italian *Inganni*. Modern scholarship has added to the list another Italian play *Gl'Ingannati* (which has characters named Fabio and Malevolti as well as a reference to Epiphany, or Twelfth Night), Italian novelle, French and English translations of the latter, Sidney's *Arcadia*, the play of *Sir Clyomon and Clamydes*, and Emanuel Forde's *Parismus* (which has the shipwreck as well as the names Olivia and Violetta). These deal in varying fashion with twins and the disguise of the girl as a page wooing in her master's behalf. As a matter of fact, Shakespeare had already used this latter device in *Two Gentlemen of Verona* with the disguised Julia in the service of her false lover Proteus.

In all these varied materials there is no suggestion of the Malvolio plot, but a possible clue as to why Shakespeare added this to the traditional materials may be found in one of the English sources, the tale of Apolonius and Silla, as related by Barnabe Riche in a collection entitled *Riche his Farewell to Militarie profession*. The reason for this rather odd title is that Riche, abandoning the wars, now prepares to devote his labors "for the onely delight of the courteous Gentlewomen bothe of England and Irelande." The story itself is remote from Shakespeare's play in many respects. Duke Apolonius, returning from war against the Turks, is forced by a storm to take refuge in Cyprus. Silla, daughter of Pontus the governor of the island, promptly falls in love with the noble visitor. After his departure for Constantinople, she sets off in pursuit accompanied by a faithful servant. After a shipwreck, Silla disguises herself and gains service as a page to Apolonius, and must then woo, on his behalf, the Lady Julina. Silla's twin brother Silvio arrives in search of his sister and is mistaken for her by Julina. Complications ensue when the impetuous Julina becomes pregnant by Silvio without benefit of wedlock. Silvio has departed in further search for his sister, but fortunately returns in time to marry Julina, while Silla wins her Apolonius.

What is more interesting to us than the story itself is the prefatory comment of Riche on the subject of love and its particular manifestations in the tale. The conventions of love were of great concern to the young ladies and gentlemen of the Queen's Court and they were aped by those beneath them in the social scale. And it is these conventions, social and literary, that Shakespeare views with Puck's amused observation — What fools these mortals be — in all three of the Joyous Comedies. Riche, however, sees no humor in his story, as his words witness:

There is no child that is borne into this wretched worlde, but before it doeth sucke the mother's milke, it taketh first a soope of the cupp of errour, which maketh us, when we come to riper yeres, not onely to enter into actions of injurie, but many tymes to straie from that is right and reason; but in all other thinges, wherein wee shewe our selves to bee moste dronken with this poisoned cuppe, it is in our actions of love; for the lover is so estranged from that is right, and wandereth so wide from the boundes of reason, that he is not able to deeme white from blacke, good from badde, vertue from vice; but onely led by the apetite of his owne affections, and groundyng them on the foolishnesse of his owne fancies, will so settle his likyng on such a one, as either by desert or unworthinesse will merite rather to be loathed then loved.

The unreasoning choice of lovers is exemplified in the story at hand, as Riche states:

Wherfore, right curteous gentilwomen, if it please you with pacience to peruse this historie following, you shall see Dame Errour so plaie her parte with a leishe of lovers, a male and twoo femalles, as shall woorke a wonder to your wise judgement, in notyng the effecte of their amorous devises and conclusions of their actions: the firste neclectyng the love of a noble dame, yong, beautifull, and faire, who onely for his good will plaied the parte of a serving manne, contented to abide any maner of paine onely to behold him: he again setting his love of a dame, that despysing hym (beeyng a noble Duke) gave her self to a servyng manne (as she had thought); but it otherwise fell out, as the substance of this tale shall better discribe.

Just what group of "curteous gentilwomen" Riche was addressing is a question. In his attitude toward love and lovers he is not following the courtly or Petrarchan tradition with its glorification of love and its absorbed interest in the subtleties of the conventions. Instead Riche, in 1581, is speaking with the harsh moralistic voice of the emerging bourgeois Puritan. In 1567 Geoffrey Fenton had translated a number of tales from the French of Belleforest with the avowed object of praising virtuous love and excoriating vice, thus hoping that "the younglings of our countrey in reding my indevor, maye break the slepe of their longe follye, and retire at last to amendement of lyfe." For Fenton, as for his French source, and for Riche, love was a disease which deprived man or woman of reason. This idea was not original with these particular authors; it had wide currency particularly in the middle class and may be traced to the classic past in Ovid's *De Remediis Amoris*, wherein that poet discusses remedies for the disease of love.

From this all too brief treatment of a large and complicated problem, it becomes clear that Riche and Shakespeare regard the story of the "leishe of lovers" from quite different points of view. Riche's use of "leishe" (leash), borrowed from the terminology of hunting and meaning a set of three hounds bound together, is sufficiently indicative of his moral scorn. For Riche the absolute folly and utter lack of rational conduct caused by love is demonstrated by the shifts which occur. Apolonius loves Julina; Julina loves the disguised Silla, who in turn loves Apolonius. At the end Apolonius marries Silla, and Julina the twin brother Silvio. Love that changes so rapidly and with so little motivation is unreasoning and senseless.

But out of this very shift in the affections Shakespeare has created the gay and charming world of Illyria. His theme is love but there the similarity with Riche ends, for Shakespeare is not interested in moral judgments; he accepts the conventions of love as they existed in the courtly world. Of course people fall in love at first sight; they always do in the love poems and romances of the age. Orsino, Viola, and Olivia all behave in thoroughly traditional fashion. In his opening scene (I, i, 20–24) Orsino describes his fall:

19

O, when mine eyes did see Olivia first,
Methought she purged the air of pestilence.
That instant was I turned into a hart,
And my desires, like fell and cruel hounds,
E'er since pursue me.

Whereas we have had some indication that the noble Duke
suffers from love's torments, we are quite unprepared, at
least by any dialogue, for Viola's sudden fall. Ordered by
Orsino to woo Olivia on his behalf, Viola acquiesces
(I, iv, 39–41):

                    I'll do my best
        To woo your lady. [aside] Yet a barful strife!
        Whoe'er I woo, myself would be his wife.

Olivia requires a few more lines than Viola to announce
her capitulation, but she is well aware of the rapidity of
the fall (I, v, 278–84).

Thy tongue, thy face, thy limbs, actions, and spirit
Do give thee fivefold blazon. Not too fast; soft, soft,
Unless the master were the man. How now?
Even so quickly may one catch the plague?
Methinks I feel this youth's perfections
With an invisible and subtle stealth
To creep in at mine eyes. Well, let it be.

The nature of the love which afflicts our characters is not
oversubtly revealed. The sophisticated Duke, well read in
love's literature, needs but one cue to pun and learnedly
compare. Concluding his apostrophe to the spirit of love,
he is asked a simple question by Curio, "Will you go hunt,
my lord?" but his seemingly simple response is well pointed
in the proper direction, "What, Curio?" The answer is the

one he wants, "The hart." Immediately Olivia becomes the hart (heart), "Why, so I do, the noblest that I have," which he pursues. At the next moment we are plunged into Ovid's *Metamorphoses* when the Duke now compares himself, after he has first seen Olivia, with Actaeon, who, having gazed on the nude Diana bathing, was punished by being transformed into a hart and pursued to death by his own hounds. Such mental agility, such appropriate references turned to the occasion of the moment were the very essence of the true courtly lover. Orsino knows the game, but Shakespeare has made him play it in seriousness.

In contrast, Olivia calmly accepts her infection with love's plague by the simple line, "Well, let it be." But this is deceptive simplicity, for properly read by a skilled actress this can be a most trenchant instance of high comedy travelling in an instant from all the conventional pretensions of her preceding lines to an amused reality.

Just such a tone distinguishes the difference in the various attitudes toward love found, for example, in I, v, where Viola goes a-wooing for Orsino. Here, particularly after the departure of Maria, when the two women are alone, we see that both are well skilled in the dialectic of love. Olivia opens with a well-known gambit, "Now, sir, what is your text?" This is the familiar association of love as a religion with its holy books, and the two play through "what chapter" to "heresy." The point of this and the subsequent dialogue is that each knows that the other is playing the game, so that this knowledge on the part of the aware spectator develops the comic value, not so much of ridicule, as amused observation of the game itself. These two can see themselves objectively but Orsino cannot, nor can Malvolio.

In the source materials of the main plot, it would seem

that Shakespeare saw the elements of high comedy. Here in a traditional story that had been told many times, always seriously, was an example of the absurdity of the literary conventions of love. As we have seen, it is with an amused eye that he views this story. At the first we have Orsino luxuriating in his own emotions; he is more in love with love than with Olivia. His opening soliloquy is too much of a good thing and would have been so recognized by a cultivated Elizabethan. This delineation of Orsino is amplified as the play progresses: in II, iv, he describes himself as a true lover, ringing the changes on the clichés; in Act V he epitomizes the eternal vacillations and improbabilities when at one moment he is prepared to kill Viola and in the next to marry her.

Similarly Olivia, having fallen in love with the disguised Viola, is perfectly willing to marry the twin brother Sebastian. If comment were needed on this sudden shift, we need only look back to Viola's analysis of the situation in II, ii. Olivia has sent Malvolio in pursuit of Viola-Cesario with a love ring, and the latter immediately recognizes what has happened:

I left no ring with her. What means this lady?
Fortune forbid my outside have not charmed her.

It is precisely with the outside, external aspects of the formalized love conventions that the main plot deals and therein lies another aspect of the humor. Nothing is serious, and after all the subtitle of the play is "What You Will."

On the other hand the subplot does approach the serious when Malvolio is imprisoned as a lunatic. Some critics have, in fact, said that Malvolio is dealt with much too harshly. It is precisely on this point that we may observe

Shakespeare's probable reason for adding the characters and incidents of this original plot to a well-known story. Love is the controlling factor in both plots but here we have a quite different set of lovers. Aguecheek is urged on by Sir Toby to think that he may win Olivia. Malvolio, tricked by the letter, but led on by his own self-love, fancies himself as suitor and husband to Olivia. In the final resolution of Act V we hear from Fabian that Sir Toby has married Maria in recompense for her writing of the letter. Now the world in which these characters function is quite different from that of Orsino, Viola and Olivia.

Sir Andrew is a mere caricature of the traditional lover, and this is pointed by the direct contrast between Sir Toby's description of him and the actuality which we see on his entrance a few lines later on. These are the attributes given him by Sir Toby: "as tall a man as any's in Illyria" ("tall" here means "brave," "outstanding"); "he plays o' th' viol-de-gamboys, and speaks three or four languages word for word without book, and hath all the good gifts of nature." If true, this description would well suit a gentleman seeking to follow the ideal of *The Courtier*. But Sir Andrew is, as Maria says, a "fool and a prodigal." Further he is stupid and vain, as his lines disclose when he completely misunderstands Sir Toby's injunction, "Accost, Sir Andrew, accost." He specifically points out his lack of knowledge of foreign languages, and though priding himself on his skill in dancing and in fencing he is last seen in I, iii, cutting a ludicrous caper, while subsequently both he and Sir Toby are given a sound beating in a fencing bout with Sebastian.

Equally apart from the tradition is Malvolio, who is early charged by Olivia with being "sick of self-love" and lacking "a free disposition." Through self-love he can naturally assume that the letter is meant for him and that it was written by the Lady Olivia. Even before he has found the letter in II, v, he is dreaming of such a marriage, but love for Malvolio has but one aspect: his own aggrandizement. He will become "Count Malvolio," will wear "some rich jewel," and Sir Toby will curtsy to him. To achieve such position and wealth he will, of course, wear yellow stockings and be ever cross-gartered. He will even attempt a free disposition and will smile.

Here then are two who have truly fallen into error, but it is not as a result of love. The fault lies rather in their own characters and attitudes toward love. Sir Andrew is fool enough to think himself a proper lover, and for his pains loses his money to Sir Toby and gets a good beating. Malvolio is presumptuous enough to think first of all that his lady would favor him and secondly that he could rise from his position as steward to that of lord of the household. Finally Sir Toby marries almost by inadvertence.

Thus the subplot may be seen as representing the obverse, the other side of the coin. In the main plot the characters move in the world of an established convention while in the other the characters are alien, if not antithetical, to the convention. We can smile with Olivia as she accepts love with "Well, let it be," or with Viola as she realizes that Olivia has fallen in love with her disguise:

> O Time, thou must untangle this, not I;
> It is too hard a knot for me t' untie.

In direct contrast with this spirit of high comedy we have the plots and trickery of low comedy where we laugh at Sir Andrew, Malvolio, and even Sir Toby, whose gulling of Sir Andrew into a duel has brought him "a bloody coxcomb." Two worlds of love and two worlds of comedy have been fused into *Twelfth Night or What You Will.*

The conventions and pretenses are not mocked in the satiric spirit, for here all is gaiety, and the lyricism which animates the play is found not only in the songs but in the characters themselves. When Viola describes how she would woo were she in love (I, v, 254–62), or tells Orsino of her concealed love (II, iv, 109–17), her lines sing with the ideal quality that is hers. So too both Orsino and Olivia reveal that they belong to the world of fancy or, in Sir Toby's words, a land of "cakes and ale" far removed from the mundane. Feste sums it all in his concluding stanza.

> A great while ago the world begun,
> With hey, ho, the wind and the rain;
> But that's all one, our play is done,
> And we'll strive to please you every day.

Yale University   CHARLES T. PROUTY

Note on the text: The only text for *Twelfth Night* is that of the folio, which appears to have been printed from the prompt copy or possibly a transcript of it. It is an excellent text, and it is here followed closely. There is some evidence that the text contains revision of the copy originally designed for performance. In the second scene Viola says that she will enter Orsino's service as his eunuch (that is, his singer) and will "speak to him in many sorts of music," but in II, iv, when Viola-Cesario is asked by Orsino to sing, she does not do so; instead Feste is sent for. Evidently the boy playing the part of Viola was not deemed an adequate singer, so that additional dialogue was written to get Feste on the stage. (There is also a possibility that Malvolio's lines at II, v, 36–37, are an interpolation, since they may refer to an event of 1616.) The act-scene division supplied marginally is that of the Globe text, which is identical with that of the folio.

Twelfth Night,
or, What You Will

[Names of the Actors

Orsino, *Duke of Illyria*
Sebastian, *brother of Viola*
Antonio, *a sea captain, friend to Sebastian*
A Sea Captain, *friend to Viola*
Valentine
Curio } *gentlemen attending on the Duke*
Sir Toby Belch, *uncle to Olivia*
Sir Andrew Aguecheek
Malvolio, *steward to Olivia*
Fabian
Feste, *a clown* } *servants to Olivia*
Olivia, *a countess*
Viola, *sister to Sebastian*
Maria, *Olivia's woman*
Lords, *a Priest, Sailors, Officers, Musicians, and Attendants*

Scene
Illyria]

TWELFTH NIGHT,
OR, WHAT YOU WILL

Enter Orsino Duke of Illyria, Curio, and other Lords,   **I, i**
    [with Musicians].

Duke. If music be the food of love, play on,
   Give me excess of it, that, surfeiting,
   The appetite may sicken, and so die.
   That strain again. It had a dying fall;
   O, it came o'er my ear like the sweet sound   **5**
   That breathes upon a bank of violets,
   Stealing and giving odor. Enough, no more.
   'Tis not so sweet now as it was before.
   O spirit of love, how quick and fresh art thou,
   That, notwithstanding thy capacity,   **10**
   Receiveth as the sea. Nought enters there,
   Of what validity and pitch soe'er,
   But falls into abatement and low price
   Even in a minute. So full of shapes is fancy
   That it alone is high fantastical.   **15**

I, i, 4 *fall* cadence   9 *quick* alive   12 *validity* value   *pitch* i.e. worth (in fal-
conry, high point of a falcon's flight)   14 *shapes* imagined forms   *fancy*
love   15 *high fantastical* highly imaginative

Curio. Will you go hunt, my lord?
Duke. What, Curio?
Curio. The hart.
Duke. Why, so I do, the noblest that I have.
20   O, when mine eyes did see Olivia first,
      Methought she purged the air of pestilence.
      That instant was I turned into a hart,
      And my desires, like fell and cruel hounds,
      E'er since pursue me.

Enter Valentine.

                    How now? What news from her?
25 *Valentine.* So please my lord, I might not be admitted;
      But from her handmaid do return this answer:
      The element itself, till seven years' heat,
      Shall not behold her face at ample view;
      But like a cloistress she will veilèd walk,
30   And water once a day her chamber round
      With eye-offending brine: all this to season
      A brother's dead love, which she would keep fresh
      And lasting in her sad remembrance.
Duke. O, she that hath a heart of that fine frame
35   To pay this debt of love but to a brother,
      How will she love when the rich golden shaft
      Hath killed the flock of all affections else
      That live in her; when liver, brain, and heart,
      These sovereign thrones, are all supplied and filled,
40   Her sweet perfections, with one self king.

22-24 *hart . . . me* (alluding to the story of Actaeon, turned into a hart by
Diana and killed by his own hounds) 23 *fell* savage 27 *element* sky *heat*
course 31 *season* preserve 36-37 *when . . . else* i.e. when Cupid's arrow
has slain all emotions except love

Away before me to sweet beds of flow'rs;
Love-thoughts lie rich when canopied with bow'rs. *Exeunt.*

Enter Viola, a Captain, and Sailors. I, ii

Viola. What country, friends, is this?
Captain. This is Illyria, lady.
Viola. And what should I do in Illyria?
My brother he is in Elysium.
Perchance he is not drowned. What think you, sailors? 5
Captain. It is perchance that you yourself were saved.
Viola. O my poor brother, and so perchance may he be.
Captain. True, madam; and, to comfort you with chance,
Assure yourself, after our ship did split,
When you, and those poor number saved with you, 10
Hung on our driving boat, I saw your brother,
Most provident in peril, bind himself
(Courage and hope both teaching him the practice)
To a strong mast that lived upon the sea;
Where, like Arion on the dolphin's back, 15
I saw him hold acquaintance with the waves
So long as I could see.
Viola. For saying so, there's gold.
Mine own escape unfoldeth to my hope,
Whereto thy speech serves for authority 20
The like of him. Know'st thou this country?

I, ii, 2 *Illyria* on the east coast of the Adriatic 4 *Elysium* home of the
blessed dead 8 *chance* what may have happened 11 *driving* drifting 14
lived floated 15 *Arion* a Greek bard who leapt overboard to escape mur-
derous sailors, and charmed dolphins with the music of his lyre so that they
bore him to land 19 *unfoldeth to my hope* gives me hope (for my brother)

Captain. Ay, madam, well, for I was bred and born
  Not three hours' travel from this very place.
Viola. Who governs here?
25 *Captain.* A noble duke, in nature as in name.
Viola. What is his name?
Captain. Orsino.
Viola. Orsino! I have heard my father name him.
  He was a bachelor then.
30 *Captain.* And so is now, or was so very late;
  For but a month ago I went from hence,
  And then 'twas fresh in murmur (as you know
  What great ones do, the less will prattle of)
  That he did seek the love of fair Olivia.
35 *Viola.* What's she?
Captain. A virtuous maid, the daughter of a count
  That died some twelvemonth since, then leaving her
  In the protection of his son, her brother,
  Who shortly also died; for whose dear love,
40   They say, she hath abjured the sight
  And company of men.
Viola.   O that I served that lady,
  And might not be delivered to the world,
  Till I had made mine own occasion mellow,
  What my estate is.
Captain.   That were hard to compass,
45   Because she will admit no kind of suit,
  No, not the Duke's.
Viola. There is a fair behavior in thee, captain,
  And though that nature with a beauteous wall
  Doth oft close in pollution, yet of thee

---

32 *fresh in murmur* a current rumor 42 *delivered* revealed 43 *mellow* ready
to be revealed 44 *estate* position in society 47 *behavior* both 'conduct'
and 'appearance'

I will believe thou hast a mind that suits   50
With this thy fair and outward character.
I prithee (and I'll pay thee bounteously)
Conceal me what I am, and be my aid
For such disguise as haply shall become
The form of my intent. I'll serve this duke.   55
Thou shalt present me as an eunuch to him;
It may be worth thy pains. For I can sing,
And speak to him in many sorts of music
That will allow me very worth his service.
What else may hap, to time I will commit;   60
Only shape thou thy silence to my wit.
Captain. Be you his eunuch, and your mute I'll be;
When my tongue blabs, then let mine eyes not see.
Viola. I thank thee. Lead me on.   *Exeunt.*

Enter Sir Toby and Maria.   I, iii

Toby. What a plague means my niece to take the death of
her brother thus? I am sure care's an enemy to life.

Maria. By my troth, Sir Toby, you must come in earlier o'
nights. Your cousin, my lady, takes great exceptions to
your ill hours.   5

Toby. Why, let her except before excepted.

Maria. Ay, but you must confine yourself within the
modest limits of order.

Toby. Confine? I'll confine myself no finer than I am.

51 *character* personal appearance indicating moral qualities   55 *form of my intent* my outward purpose   56 *eunuch* i.e. singer (but she enters his service simply as a page)   59 *allow me* cause me to be considered   I, iii, 4 *cousin* kinsman   6 *except before excepted* (cant legal phrase)   9 *finer* both 'tighter' and 'better'

10 These clothes are good enough to drink in, and so be
    these boots too. An they be not, let them hang them-
    selves in their own straps.

Maria. That quaffing and drinking will undo you. I heard
    my lady talk of it yesterday; and of a foolish knight that
15 you brought in one night here to be her wooer.

Toby. Who? Sir Andrew Aguecheek?

Maria. Ay, he.

Toby. He's as tall a man as any's in Illyria.

Maria. What's that to th' purpose?

20 *Toby.* Why, he has three thousand ducats a year.

Maria. Ay, but he'll have but a year in all these ducats. He's
    a very fool and a prodigal.

Toby. Fie that you'll say so! He plays o' th' viol-de-gam-
    boys, and speaks three or four languages word for word
25 without book, and hath all the good gifts of nature.

Maria. He hath, indeed, almost natural; for, besides that
    he's a fool, he's a great quarreller; and but that he hath
    the gift of a coward to allay the gust he hath in quarrel-
    ling, 'tis thought among the prudent he would quickly
30 have the gift of a grave.

Toby. By this hand, they are scoundrels and substractors
    that say so of him. Who are they?

Maria. They that add, moreover, he's drunk nightly in your
    company.

35 *Toby.* With drinking healths to my niece. I'll drink to her
    as long as there is a passage in my throat and drink in
    Illyria. He's a coward and a coistrel that will not drink to

---

11 *An* if   18 *tall* both 'tall' and 'brave'   23–24 *viol-de-gamboys* 'leg-viola,'
predecessor of the violoncello   25 *without book* by memory   26 *natural*
i.e. as a fool   28 *gust* taste   31 *substractors* detractors   37 *coistrel* horse-
groom, base fellow

my niece till his brains turn o' th' toe like a parish top.
What, wench? Castiliano vulgo; for here comes Sir
Andrew Agueface.   40

Enter Sir Andrew.

Andrew. Sir Toby Belch. How now, Sir Toby Belch?
Toby. Sweet Sir Andrew.
Andrew. Bless you, fair shrew.
Maria. And you too, sir.
Toby. Accost, Sir Andrew, accost.   45
Andrew. What's that?
Toby. My niece's chambermaid.
Andrew. Good Mistress Accost, I desire better acquaintance.
Maria. My name is Mary, sir.
Andrew. Good Mistress Mary Accost.   50
Toby. You mistake, knight. 'Accost' is front her, board her,
   woo her, assail her.
Andrew. By my troth, I would not undertake her in this
   company. Is that the meaning of 'accost'?
Maria. Fare you well, gentlemen.   55
Toby. An thou let part so, Sir Andrew, would thou mightst
   never draw sword again.
Andrew. An you part so, mistress, I would I might never
   draw sword again! Fair lady, do you think you have
   fools in hand?   60
Maria. Sir, I have not you by th' hand.

---

38 *parish* kept by the parish (?)   39 *Castiliano vulgo* (of doubtful meaning.
Castilians were noted for decorum, and this may be a plea for 'common
politeness.')   40 *Agueface* pale and thin-faced, like a man suffering from the
acute fever of ague   45 *Accost* make up to (her)   51 *front* face   *board* greet
(literally, go on board)   53 *undertake* (both literal and figurative senses intended)

Andrew. Marry, but you shall have, and here's my hand.

Maria. Now, sir, thought is free. I pray you, bring your
hand to th' butt'ry bar and let it drink.

65 *Andrew.* Wherefore, sweetheart? What's your metaphor?

Maria. It's dry, sir.

Andrew. Why, I think so. I am not such an ass but I can
keep my hand dry. But what's your jest?

Maria. A dry jest, sir.

70 *Andrew.* Are you full of them?

Maria. Ay, sir, I have them at my fingers' ends. Marry, now
I let go your hand, I am barren.   *Exit.*

Toby. O knight, thou lack'st a cup of canary! When did I
see thee so put down?

75 *Andrew.* Never in your life, I think, unless you see canary
put me down. Methinks sometimes I have no more wit
than a Christian or an ordinary man has. But I am a great
eater of beef, and I believe that does harm to my wit.

Toby. No question.

80 *Andrew.* An I thought that, I'd forswear it. I'll ride home
to-morrow, Sir Toby.

Toby. Pourquoi, my dear knight?

Andrew. What is 'pourquoi'? Do, or not do? I would I had
bestowed that time in the tongues that I have in fencing,
85 dancing, and bear-baiting. O, had I but followed the arts!

Toby. Then hadst thou had an excellent head of hair.

Andrew. Why, would that have mended my hair?

Toby. Past question, for thou seest it will not curl by
nature.

---

62 *Marry* indeed, to be sure (originally an oath by the Virgin Mary) 64
butt'ry ale-cellar *it* i.e. your hand 66 *dry* (a sign of age) 72 *barren* i.e.
barren of jokes 73 *canary* a sweet wine from the Canary Islands 74 *put
down* discomfited 82 *Pourquoi* why 84 *tongues* languages, perhaps with
a pun on 'tongs,' curling irons 85 *arts* liberal arts such as languages 87
mended improved

Andrew. But it becomes me well enough, does't not?   90

Toby. Excellent. It hangs like flax on a distaff; and I hope
to see a housewife take thee between her legs and spin it
off.

Andrew. Faith, I'll home to-morrow, Sir Toby. Your niece
will not be seen; or if she be, it's four to one she'll none   95
of me. The Count himself here hard by woos her.

Toby. She'll none o' th' Count. She'll not match above her
degree, neither in estate, years, nor wit; I have heard her
swear't. Tut, there's life in't, man.

Andrew. I'll stay a month longer. I am a fellow o' th'   100
strangest mind i' th' world. I delight in masques and
revels sometimes altogether.

Toby. Art thou good at these kickshawses, knight?

Andrew. As any man in Illyria, whatsoever he be, under the
degree of my betters, and yet I will not compare with an   105
old man.

Toby. What is thy excellence in a galliard, knight?

Andrew. Faith, I can cut a caper.

Toby. And I can cut the mutton to't.

Andrew. And I think I have the back-trick simply as strong   110
as any man in Illyria.

Toby. Wherefore are these things hid? Wherefore have
these gifts a curtain before 'em? Are they like to take
dust, like Mistress Mall's picture? Why dost thou not go
to church in a galliard and come home in a coranto? My   115
very walk should be a jig. I would not so much as make

91 *flax on a distaff* straight strings of flax on a stick used in spinning 98
degree position in society *estate* fortune 102 *altogether* in all respects 103
kickshawses trifles (French *quelque chose*) 106 *old man* probably 'experi-
enced person' 107 *galliard* quick dance in triple time 108 *caper* frolic-
some leap; also a spice used with mutton 110 *back-trick* backward step in
a dance 113 *take* collect 114 *Mistress Mall's picture* any woman's portrait
115 *coranto* swift running dance

water but in a sink-a-pace. What dost thou mean? Is it a
world to hide virtues in? I did think, by the excellent
constitution of thy leg, it was formed under the star of a
120　galliard.

Andrew. Ay, 'tis strong, and it does indifferent well in a
flame-colored stock. Shall we set about some revels?

Toby. What shall we do else? Were we not born under
Taurus?

125　*Andrew.* Taurus? That's sides and heart.

Toby. No, sir; it is legs and thighs. Let me see thee caper.
Ha, higher; ha, ha, excellent!　　　　　　　*Exeunt.*

I, iv　　　　*Enter Valentine, and Viola in man's attire.*

Valentine. If the Duke continue these favors towards you,
Cesario, you are like to be much advanced. He hath known
you but three days and already you are no stranger.

Viola. You either fear his humor or my negligence, that
5　you call in question the continuance of his love. Is he
inconstant, sir, in his favors?

Valentine. No, believe me.

Enter Duke, Curio, and Attendants.

Viola. I thank you. Here comes the Count.

Duke. Who saw Cesario, ho?

10　*Viola.* On your attendance, my lord, here.

Duke. Stand you awhile aloof. Cesario,

---

117 *sink-a-pace* rapid dance of five steps (French *cinque-pas*)　119–20 *under
. . . galliard* i.e. under a dancing star　122 *stock* stocking　124 *Taurus* the
Bull, one of the signs of the Zodiac　I, iv, 4 *humor* changeableness　11
you i.e. all except Cesario

Thou know'st no less but all. I have unclasped
To thee the book even of my secret soul.
Therefore, good youth, address thy gait unto her;
Be not denied access, stand at her doors,   15
And tell them there thy fixèd foot shall grow
Till thou have audience.

Viola.   Sure, my noble lord,
If she be so abandoned to her sorrow
As it is spoke, she never will admit me.

Duke. Be clamorous and leap all civil bounds   20
Rather than make unprofited return.

Viola. Say I do speak with her, my lord, what then?

Duke. O, then unfold the passion of my love;
Surprise her with discourse of my dear faith;
It shall become thee well to act my woes.   25
She will attend it better in thy youth
Than in a nuncio's of more grave aspect.

Viola. I think not so, my lord.

Duke.   Dear lad, believe it;
For they shall yet belie thy happy years
That say thou art a man. Diana's lip   30
Is not more smooth and rubious; thy small pipe
Is as the maiden's organ, shrill and sound,
And all is semblative a woman's part.
I know thy constellation is right apt
For this affair. Some four or five attend him,   35
All, if you will; for I myself am best
When least in company. Prosper well in this,
And thou shalt live as freely as thy lord
To call his fortunes thine.

12 *no less but all* everything 14 *address thy gait* direct your steps 27 *nuncio's* messenger's 31 *rubious* ruby red *pipe* throat, voice 32 *shrill and sound* high and clear 33 *semblative* like 34 *constellation* predestined nature

Viola.   I'll do my best

40   To woo your lady. *[aside]* Yet a barful strife!

Whoe'er I woo, myself would be his wife.   *Exeunt.*

I, v   *Enter Maria and Clown.*

Maria. Nay, either tell me where thou hast been, or I will
not open my lips so wide as a bristle may enter in way of
thy excuse. My lady will hang thee for thy absence.

Clown. Let her hang me. He that is well hanged in this
5   world needs to fear no colors.

Maria. Make that good.

Clown. He shall see none to fear.

Maria. A good lenten answer. I can tell thee where that
saying was born, of 'I fear no colors.'

10 *Clown.* Where, good Mistress Mary?

Maria. In the wars; and that may you be bold to say in your
foolery.

Clown. Well, God give them wisdom that have it, and
those that are fools, let them use their talents.

15 *Maria.* Yet you will be hanged for being so long absent, or
to be turned away. Is not that as good as a hanging to
you?

Clown. Many a good hanging prevents a bad marriage, and
for turning away, let summer bear it out.

20 *Maria.* Are you resolute then?

Clown. Not so, neither; but I am resolved on two points.

---

40 *barful strife* conflict full of hindrances   I, v, 5 *fear no colors* fear nothing
(proverbial)   8 *lenten* thin, scanty   19 *let . . . out* i.e. let mild weather make
homelessness endurable

Maria. That if one break, the other will hold; or if both break, your gaskins fall.

Clown. Apt, in good faith; very apt. Well, go thy way! If Sir Toby would leave drinking, thou wert as witty a piece 25 of Eve's flesh as any in Illyria.

Maria. Peace, you rogue; no more o' that. Here comes my lady. Make your excuse wisely, you were best. *[Exit.]*

Enter Lady Olivia with Malvolio.

Clown. Wit, an't be thy will, put me into good fooling. Those wits that think they have thee do very oft prove 30 fools, and I that am sure I lack thee may pass for a wise man. For what says Quinapalus? 'Better a witty fool than a foolish wit.' God bless thee, lady.

Olivia. Take the fool away.

Clown. Do you not hear, fellows? Take away the lady. 35

Olivia. Go to, y' are a dry fool! I'll no more of you. Besides, you grow dishonest.

Clown. Two faults, madonna, that drink and good counsel will amend. For give the dry fool drink, then is the fool not dry. Bid the dishonest man mend himself: if he 40 mend, he is no longer dishonest; if he cannot, let the botcher mend him. Anything that's mended is but patched; virtue that transgresses is but patched with sin, and sin that amends is but patched with virtue. If that this simple syllogism will serve, so; if it will not, what 45 remedy? As there is no true cuckold but calamity, so beauty's a flower. The lady bade take away the fool; therefore, I say again, take her away.

22–23 *if one . . . fall* (Maria puns on *points* = laces used to hold up breeches) 23 *gaskins* loose breeches 28 *you were best* it would be best for you 32 *Quinapalus* (an invention of the Clown) 36 *Go to* enough, cease *dry* dull 37 *dishonest* unreliable 38 *madonna* my lady 40 *dry* thirsty 42 *botcher* mender of clothes

Olivia. Sir, I bade them take away you.

50 *Clown.* Misprision in the highest degree. Lady, cucullus non facit monachum. That's as much to say as, I wear not motley in my brain. Good madonna, give me leave to prove you a fool.

Olivia. Can you do it?

55 *Clown.* Dexteriously, good madonna.

Olivia. Make your proof.

Clown. I must catechize you for it, madonna. Good my mouse of virtue, answer me.

Olivia. Well, sir, for want of other idleness, I'll bide your
60 proof.

Clown. Good madonna, why mourn'st thou?

Olivia. Good fool, for my brother's death.

Clown. I think his soul is in hell, madonna.

Olivia. I know his soul is in heaven, fool.

65 *Clown.* The more fool, madonna, to mourn for your brother's soul, being in heaven. Take away the fool, gentlemen.

Olivia. What think you of this fool, Malvolio? Doth he not mend?

70 *Malvolio.* Yes, and shall do till the pangs of death shake him. Infirmity, that decays the wise, doth ever make the better fool.

Clown. God send you, sir, a speedy infirmity, for the better increasing your folly. Sir Toby will be sworn that I am
75 no fox, but he will not pass his word for twopence that you are no fool.

Olivia. How say you to that, Malvolio?

---

50 *Misprision* error 50–51 *cucullus . . . monachum* the cowl doesn't make the monk 52 *motley* clothing of a mixed color, worn by stage fools 55 *Dexteriously* (variant of *dexterously*) 58 *mouse* (term of endearment) *of virtue* virtuous

Malvolio. I marvel your ladyship takes delight in such a
barren rascal. I saw him put down the other day with an
ordinary fool that has no more brain than a stone. Look 80
you now, he's out of his guard already. Unless you laugh
and minister occasion to him, he is gagged. I protest I take
these wise men that crow so at these set kind of fools no
better than the fools' zanies.

Olivia. O, you are sick of self-love, Malvolio, and taste with 85
a distempered appetite. To be generous, guiltless, and of
free disposition, is to take those things for birdbolts that
you deem cannon bullets. There is no slander in an
allowed fool, though he do nothing but rail; nor no
railing in a known discreet man, though he do nothing 90
but reprove.

Clown. Now Mercury indue thee with leasing, for thou
speak'st well of fools.

Enter Maria.

Maria. Madam, there is at the gate a young gentleman
much desires to speak with you.   95

Olivia. From the Count Orsino, is it?

Maria. I know not, madam. 'Tis a fair young man, and well
attended.

Olivia. Who of my people hold him in delay?

Maria. Sir Toby, madam, your kinsman.   100

Olivia. Fetch him off, I pray you. He speaks nothing but
madman. Fie on him! *[Exit Maria.]* Go you, Malvolio.
If it be a suit from the Count, I am sick, or not at home.
What you will, to dismiss it. *(Exit Malvolio.)* Now you

81 *out of his guard* without a defense (of wit)   84 *zanies* fools' assistants
87 *birdbolts* blunt-headed arrows for shooting birds   89 *allowed* licensed
92 *Mercury* god of guile and tricks   *indue . . . leasing* endow you with the
art of casuistry

105   see, sir, how your fooling grows old, and people dislike
it.

Clown. Thou hast spoke for us, madonna, as if thy eldest
son should be a fool; whose skull Jove cram with brains,
for — here he comes — one of thy kin has a most weak
110   pia mater.

Enter Sir Toby.

Olivia. By mine honor, half drunk. What is he at the gate,
cousin?

Toby. A gentleman.

Olivia. A gentleman? What gentleman?

115 *Toby.* 'Tis a gentleman here. A plague o' these pickle-
herring! How now, sot?

Clown. Good Sir Toby.

Olivia. Cousin, cousin, how have you come so early by
this lethargy?

120 *Toby.* Lechery? I defy lechery. There's one at the gate.

Olivia. Ay, marry, what is he?

Toby. Let him be the devil an he will, I care not. Give me
faith, say I. Well, it's all one.   *Exit.*

Olivia. What's a drunken man like, fool?

125 *Clown.* Like a drowned man, a fool, and a madman. One
draught above heat makes him a fool, the second mads
him, and a third drowns him.

Olivia. Go thou and seek the crowner, and let him sit o' my
coz; for he's in the third degree of drink — he's drowned.
130   Go look after him.

---

105 *old* stale   110 *pia mater* i.e. brain   123 *faith* i.e. to resist the devil   126
above heat above the amount to make him normally warm   128 *crowner*
coroner   128–29 *sit o' my coz* hold an inquest on my kinsman (Sir Toby)

Clown. He is but mad yet, madonna, and the fool shall look
to the madman.   *[Exit.]*

Enter Malvolio.

Malvolio. Madam, yond young fellow swears he will speak
with you. I told him you were sick; he takes on him to
understand so much, and therefore comes to speak with 135
you. I told him you were asleep; he seems to have a fore-
knowledge of that too, and therefore comes to speak
with you. What is to be said to him, lady? He's fortified
against any denial.

Olivia. Tell him he shall not speak with me.   140

Malvolio. Has been told so; and he says he'll stand at your
door like a sheriff's post, and be the supporter to a bench,
but he'll speak with you.

Olivia. What kind o' man is he?

Malvolio. Why, of mankind.   145

Olivia. What manner of man?

Malvolio. Of very ill manner. He'll speak with you, will
you or no.

Olivia. Of what personage and years is he?

Malvolio. Not yet old enough for a man nor young enough 150
for a boy; as a squash is before 'tis a peascod, or a codling
when 'tis almost an apple. 'Tis with him in standing
water, between boy and man. He is very well-favored
and he speaks very shrewishly. One would think his
mother's milk were scarce out of him.   155

---

141 *Has* he has (from 'h' has')   142 *sheriff's post* post before a sheriff's
house on which notices were posted   151 *squash* unripe pea pod   *peascod*
ripe pea pod   *codling* unripe apple   152–53 *standing water* the tide at ebb or
flood when it flows neither way

Olivia. Let him approach. Call in my gentlewoman.
Malvolio. Gentlewoman, my lady calls.   **Exit.**

Enter Maria.

Olivia. Give me my veil; come, throw it o'er my face.
We'll once more hear Orsino's embassy.

Enter Viola.

160 *Viola.* The honorable lady of the house, which is she?
Olivia. Speak to me; I shall answer for her. Your will?
Viola. Most radiant, exquisite, and unmatchable beauty – I
    pray you tell me if this be the lady of the house, for I
    never saw her. I would be loath to cast away my speech;
165   for, besides that it is excellently well penned, I have
    taken great pains to con it. Good beauties, let me sustain
    no scorn. I am very comptible, even to the least sinister
    usage.
Olivia. Whence came you, sir?
170 *Viola.* I can say little more than I have studied, and that
    question's out of my part. Good gentle one, give me
    modest assurance if you be the lady of the house, that I
    may proceed in my speech.
Olivia. Are you a comedian?
175 *Viola.* No, my profound heart; and yet (by the very fangs
    of malice I swear) I am not that I play. Are you the
    lady of the house?
Olivia. If I do not usurp myself, I am.
Viola. Most certain, if you are she, you do usurp yourself;
180   for what is yours to bestow is not yours to reserve. But
    this is from my commission. I will on with my speech in
    your praise and then show you the heart of my message.

166 *con* memorize *sustain* endure 167 *comptible* sensitive 174 *comedian*
actor 178 *usurp* supplant 181 *from* outside

Olivia. Come to what is important in't. I forgive you the
praise.

Viola. Alas, I took great pains to study it, and 'tis poetical. 185

Olivia. It is the more like to be feigned; I pray you keep it
in. I heard you were saucy at my gates; and allowed your
approach rather to wonder at you than to hear you. If
you be not mad, be gone; if you have reason, be brief.
'Tis not that time of moon with me to make one in so 190
skipping a dialogue.

Maria. Will you hoist sail, sir? Here lies your way.

Viola. No, good swabber; I am to hull here a little longer.
Some mollification for your giant, sweet lady. Tell me
your mind. I am a messenger.   195

Olivia. Sure you have some hideous matter to deliver,
when the courtesy of it is so fearful. Speak your office.

Viola. It alone concerns your ear. I bring no overture of
war, no taxation of homage. I hold the olive in my hand.
My words are as full of peace as matter.   200

Olivia. Yet you began rudely. What are you? What would
you?

Viola. The rudeness that hath appeared in me have I
learned from my entertainment. What I am, and what I
would, are as secret as maidenhead: to your ears, divin- 205
ity; to any other's, profanation.

Olivia. Give us the place alone; we will hear this divinity.
[*Exit Maria.*] Now, sir, what is your text?

Viola. Most sweet lady —

Olivia. A comfortable doctrine, and much may be said of 210
it. Where lies your text?

183 *forgive* excuse 189 *reason* sanity 190 *'Tis . . . me* i.e. I am not in the
mood 191 *skipping* sprightly 193 *swabber* one who washes decks *hull*
float without sail 194 *giant* i.e. the small Maria 197 *courtesy* formality
office business 199 *taxation* demand 204 *entertainment* reception 205–6
divinity a holy message

47

Viola. In Orsino's bosom.

Olivia. In his bosom? In what chapter of his bosom?

Viola. To answer by the method, in the first of his heart.

215 *Olivia.* O, I have read it; it is heresy. Have you no more
to say?

Viola. Good madam, let me see your face.

Olivia. Have you any commission from your lord to ne-
gotiate with my face? You are now out of your text.

220 But we will draw the curtain and show you the picture.
[Unveils.] Look you, sir, such a one I was this present.
Is't not well done?

Viola. Excellently done, if God did all.

Olivia. 'Tis in grain, sir; 'twill endure wind and weather.

225 *Viola.* 'Tis beauty truly blent, whose red and white
Nature's own sweet and cunning hand laid on.
Lady, you are the cruell'st she alive
If you will lead these graces to the grave,
And leave the world no copy.

230 *Olivia.* O, sir, I will not be so hard-hearted. I will give out
divers schedules of my beauty. It shall be inventoried, and
every particle and utensil labelled to my will: as, item,
two lips, indifferent red; item, two grey eyes, with lids
to them; item, one neck, one chin, and so forth. Were
235 you sent hither to praise me?

Viola. I see you what you are; you are too proud;
But if you were the devil, you are fair.
My lord and master loves you. O, such love
Could be but recompensed though you were crowned
The nonpareil of beauty.

---

221 *this present* a minute ago 224 *in grain* fast dyed 226 *cunning* skillful
231 *schedules* lists 232 *utensil* article *labelled to* added to *item* namely
233 *indifferent* moderately 237 *if* even if 239 *but recompensed though* no
more than repaid even though

48

Olivia.   How does he love me?   240
Viola. With adorations, with fertile tears,
   With groans that thunder love, with sighs of fire.
Olivia. Your lord does know my mind; I cannot love him.
   Yet I suppose him virtuous, know him noble,
   Of great estate, of fresh and stainless youth;   245
   In voices well divulged, free, learned, and valiant,
   And in dimension and the shape of nature
   A gracious person. But yet I cannot love him.
   He might have took his answer long ago.
Viola. If I did love you in my master's flame,   250
   With such a suff'ring, such a deadly life,
   In your denial I would find no sense;
   I would not understand it.
Olivia.   Why, what would you?
Viola. Make me a willow cabin at your gate
   And call upon my soul within the house;   255
   Write loyal cantons of contemnèd love
   And sing them loud even in the dead of night;
   Hallo your name to the reverberate hills
   And make the babbling gossip of the air
   Cry out 'Olivia!' O, you should not rest   260
   Between the elements of air and earth
   But you should pity me.
Olivia. You might do much. What is your parentage?
Viola. Above my fortunes, yet my state is well.
   I am a gentleman.
Olivia.   Get you to your lord.   265
   I cannot love him. Let him send no more,

241 *fertile* abundant 246 *In voices well divulged* in public opinion well re-
ported 251 *deadly life* life which is like death 254 *willow* symbol of grief
for unrequited love 256 *cantons* songs *contemnèd* rejected 259 *babbling
gossip* echo

    Unless, perchance, you come to me again
    To tell me how he takes it. Fare you well.
    I thank you for your pains. Spend this for me.
270 *Viola.* I am no fee'd post, lady; keep your purse;
    My master, not myself, lacks recompense.
    Love make his heart of flint that you shall love;
    And let your fervor, like my master's, be
    Placed in contempt. Farewell, fair cruelty.   *Exit.*
275 *Olivia.* 'What is your parentage?'
    'Above my fortunes, yet my state is well.
    I am a gentleman.' I'll be sworn thou art.
    Thy tongue, thy face, thy limbs, actions, and spirit
    Do give thee fivefold blazon. Not too fast; soft, soft,
280 Unless the master were the man. How now?
    Even so quickly may one catch the plague?
    Methinks I feel this youth's perfections
    With an invisible and subtle stealth
    To creep in at mine eyes. Well, let it be.
    What ho, Malvolio!

Enter Malvolio.

285 *Malvolio.*   Here, madam, at your service.
    Olivia. Run after that same peevish messenger,
    The County's man. He left this ring behind him,
    Would I or not. Tell him I'll none of it.
    Desire him not to flatter with his lord
290 Nor hold him up with hopes. I am not for him.
    If that the youth will come this way to-morrow,
    I'll give him reasons for't. Hie thee, Malvolio.
    Malvolio. Madam, I will.   *Exit.*

---

270 *fee'd post* messenger to be paid or tipped   279 *blazon* shield or coat of arms in heraldry   280 *Unless . . . man* i.e. unless Orsino were Cesario   287 *County* count   289 *flatter with* encourage

Olivia. I do know not what, and fear to find
    Mine eye too great a flatterer for my mind.   295
    Fate, show thy force; ourselves we do not owe.
    What is decreed must be — and be this so!   *[Exit.]*

Enter Antonio and Sebastian.   II, i

Antonio. Will you stay no longer? Nor will you not that I
    go with you?

Sebastian. By your patience, no. My stars shine darkly over
    me; the malignancy of my fate might perhaps distemper
    yours. Therefore I shall crave of you your leave, that I 5
    may bear my evils alone. It were a bad recompense for
    your love to lay any of them on you.

Antonio. Let me yet know of you whither you are bound.

Sebastian. No, sooth, sir. My determinate voyage is mere
    extravagancy. But I perceive in you so excellent a touch 10
    of modesty that you will not extort from me what I am
    willing to keep in; therefore it charges me in manners the
    rather to express myself. You must know of me then,
    Antonio, my name is Sebastian, which I called Roderigo.
    My father was that Sebastian of Messaline whom I know 15
    you have heard of. He left behind him myself and a
    sister, both born in an hour. If the heavens had been
    pleased, would we had so ended! But you, sir, altered
    that, for some hour before you took me from the breach
    of the sea was my sister drowned.   20

Antonio. Alas the day!

296 *owe* own II, i, 3 *patience* leave 9 *sooth* truly *determinate* determined
upon 10 *extravagancy* wandering 12 *it . . . manners* I am compelled in
good manners 17 *in an hour* in the same hour 19–20 *the breach of the
sea* the breaking waves

Sebastian. A lady, sir, though it was said she much resem-
bled me, was yet of many accounted beautiful. But
though I could not with such estimable wonder overfar
25 believe that, yet thus far I will boldly publish her: she
bore a mind that envy could not but call fair. She is
drowned already, sir, with salt water, though I seem to
drown her remembrance again with more.

Antonio. Pardon me, sir, your bad entertainment.

30 *Sebastian.* O good Antonio, forgive me your trouble.

Antonio. If you will not murder me for my love, let me be
your servant.

Sebastian. If you will not undo what you have done, that is,
kill him whom you have recovered, desire it not. Fare ye
35 well at once. My bosom is full of kindness, and I am yet
so near the manners of my mother that, upon the least
occasion more, mine eyes will tell tales of me. I am bound
to the Count Orsino's court. Farewell.   *Exit.*

Antonio. The gentleness of all the gods go with thee.
40 I have many enemies in Orsino's court,
Else would I very shortly see thee there.
But come what may, I do adore thee so
That danger shall seem sport, and I will go.   *Exit.*

II, ii   *Enter Viola and Malvolio at several doors.*

Malvolio. Were not you ev'n now with the Countess
Olivia?

---

24 *estimable wonder* admiring judgment   25 *publish* describe publicly   29
entertainment treatment as my guest   30 *your trouble* for causing you trouble
31 *murder me for* be my death in return for   34 *recovered* saved   36–37 *so
near . . . tales of me* so effeminate I shall weep   II, ii, S.D. *several* different

Viola. Even now, sir. On a moderate pace I have since
arrived but hither.

Malvolio. She returns this ring to you, sir. You might have 5
saved me my pains, to have taken it away yourself. She
adds, moreover, that you should put your lord into a desperate assurance she will none of him. And one thing
more, that you be never so hardy to come again in his
affairs, unless it be to report your lord's taking of this. 10
Receive it so.

Viola. She took the ring of me. I'll none of it.

Malvolio. Come, sir, you peevishly threw it to her, and her
will is, it should be so returned. If it be worth stooping
for, there it lies, in your eye; if not, be it his that finds it. 15

Exit.

Viola. I left no ring with her. What means this lady?
Fortune forbid my outside have not charmed her.
She made good view of me; indeed, so much
That, as methought, her eyes had lost her tongue,
For she did speak in starts distractedly. 20
She loves me sure; the cunning of her passion
Invites me in this churlish messenger.
None of my lord's ring? Why, he sent her none.
I am the man. If it be so, as 'tis,
Poor lady, she were better love a dream. 25
Disguise, I see thou art a wickedness
Wherein the pregnant enemy does much.
How easy is it for the proper false
In women's waxen hearts to set their forms!
Alas, our frailty is the cause, not we, 30

7–8 *desperate* without hope 18 *made good view of* looked intently at 19 *lost*
caused her to lose 21 *cunning* craftiness 27 *pregnant enemy* resourceful
Satan 28 *the proper false* deceivers who are prepossessing in appearance
29 *forms* impressions (as of a seal)

For such as we are made of, such we be.
How will this fadge? My master loves her dearly;
And I (poor monster) fond as much on him;
And she (mistaken) seems to dote on me.
35 What will become of this? As I am man,
My state is desperate for my master's love.
As I am woman (now alas the day!),
What thriftless sighs shall poor Olivia breathe?
O Time, thou must untangle this, not I;
40 It is too hard a knot for me t' untie.   *[Exit.]*

II, iii   *Enter Sir Toby and Sir Andrew.*

Toby. Approach, Sir Andrew. Not to be abed after midnight is to be up betimes; and 'diluculo surgere,' thou
know'st.

Andrew. Nay, by my troth, I know not, but I know to be
5 up late is to be up late.

Toby. A false conclusion; I hate it as an unfilled can. To be
up after midnight, and to go to bed then, is early; so that
to go to bed after midnight is to go to bed betimes. Does
not our lives consist of the four elements?

10 *Andrew.* Faith, so they say; but I think it rather consists of
eating and drinking.

---

32 *fadge* be suitable 33 *monster* (because both man and woman) *fond* dote
36 *desperate* hopeless 38 *thriftless* unprofitable II, iii, 2 *diluculo surgere*
[*saluberrimum est*] to get up at dawn is healthful (Lily's *Latin Grammar*)
6 *can* metal vessel for holding liquor

Toby. Th' art a scholar! Let us therefore eat and drink.
Marian I say! a stoup of wine!

Enter Clown.

Andrew. Here comes the fool, i' faith.

Clown. How now, my hearts? Did you never see the pic- 15
ture of We Three?

Toby. Welcome, ass. Now let's have a catch.

Andrew. By my troth, the fool has an excellent breast. I had
rather than forty shillings I had such a leg, and so sweet a
breath to sing, as the fool has. In sooth, thou wast in very 20
gracious fooling last night, when thou spok'st of Pigrogromitus, of the Vapians passing the equinoctial of
Queubus. 'Twas very good, i' faith. I sent thee sixpence
for thy leman. Hadst it?

Clown. I did impeticos thy gratillity, for Malvolio's nose is 25
no whipstock. My lady has a white hand, and the Myrmidons are no bottle-ale houses.

Andrew. Excellent. Why, this is the best fooling, when all
is done. Now a song!

Toby. Come on! there is sixpence for you. Let's have a song. 30

Andrew. There's a testril of me too. If one knight give a –

Clown. Would you have a love song, or a song of good
life?

Toby. A love song, a love song.

Andrew. Ay, ay, I care not for good life.   35

13 *stoup* goblet   15 *hearts* (term of endearment)   15–16 *picture of We
Three* picture showing two fools or asses inscribed 'we three,' the onlooker
making the third   17 *catch* round-song (such as 'Three Blind Mice')   18
breast voice   21 *gracious* elegant   21–23 *Pigrogromitus . . . Queubus* (mean-
ingless mock-learning)   24 *leman* sweetheart   25 *impeticos* put in pocket of
gown   *gratillity* gratuity   26–27 *Myrmidons* Thessalian warriors (meaning-
less here)   31 *testril* tester, sixpence   32–33 *good life* virtuous living

Clown sings.

O mistress mine, where are you roaming?
O, stay and hear! your true-love's coming,
  That can sing both high and low.
Trip no further, pretty sweeting;
40 Journeys end in lovers meeting,
  Every wise man's son doth know.

Andrew. Excellent good, i' faith.
Toby. Good, good.

Clown [sings].

What is love? 'Tis not hereafter;
45 Present mirth hath present laughter;
  What's to come is still unsure:
In delay there lies no plenty;
Then come kiss me, sweet and twenty,
  Youth's a stuff will not endure.

50 *Andrew.* A mellifluous voice, as I am true knight.
Toby. A contagious breath.
Andrew. Very sweet and contagious, i' faith.
Toby. To hear by the nose, it is dulcet in contagion. But
  shall we make the welkin dance indeed? Shall we rouse
55 the night owl in a catch that will draw three souls out of
  one weaver? Shall we do that?
Andrew. An you love me, let's do't. I am dog at a catch.
Clown. By'r Lady, sir, and some dogs will catch well.
Andrew. Most certain. Let our catch be 'Thou knave.'
60 *Clown.* 'Hold thy peace, thou knave,' knight? I shall be
  constrained in't to call thee knave, knight.
Andrew. 'Tis not the first time I have constrained one to
  call me knave. Begin, fool. It begins, 'Hold thy peace.'

54 *welkin* sky   56 *weaver* (weavers were famous for singing)

Clown. I shall never begin if I hold my peace.

Andrew. Good, i' faith! Come, begin.   65

Catch sung. Enter Maria.

Maria. What a caterwauling do you keep here? If my lady
have not called up her steward Malvolio and bid him turn
you out of doors, never trust me.

Toby. My lady's a Cataian, we are politicians, Malvolio's a
Peg-a-Ramsey, and *[sings]* 'Three merry men be we.'   70
Am not I consanguineous? Am I not of her blood?
Tilly-vally, lady. *[sings]* 'There dwelt a man in Babylon,
lady, lady.'

Clown. Beshrew me, the knight's in admirable fooling.

Andrew. Ay, he does well enough if he be disposed, and so   75
do I too. He does it with a better grace, but I do it more
natural.

Toby. *[sings]* 'O the twelfth day of December.'

Maria. For the love o' God, peace!

Enter Malvolio.

Malvolio. My masters, are you mad? Or what are you?   80
Have you no wit, manners, nor honesty, but to gabble
like tinkers at this time of night? Do ye make an alehouse
of my lady's house, that ye squeak out your coziers'
catches without any mitigation or remorse of voice? Is
there no respect of place, persons, nor time in you?   85

Toby. We did keep time, sir, in our catches. Sneck up.

Malvolio. Sir Toby, I must be round with you. My lady

69 *Cataian* native of Cathay, trickster   *politicians* intriguers   70 *Peg-a-
Ramsey* character in an old song, here used as a term of contempt   71 *consanguineous* related   72 *Tilly-vally* nonsense   72–73 *There dwelt . . .* (from
an old song, 'The Constancy of Susanna')   77 *natural* naturally (but the
word also means 'like a fool')   83 *coziers'* cobblers'   84 *mitigation or remorse* i.e. considerate lowering   86 *Sneck up* go hang   87 *round* plain

bade me tell you that, though she harbors you as her kinsman, she's nothing allied to your disorders. If you can
90   separate yourself and your misdemeanors, you are welcome to the house. If not, and it would please you to take
leave of her, she is very willing to bid you farewell.

Toby. *[sings]* 'Farewell, dear heart since I must needs be
gone.'

Maria. Nay, good Sir Toby.

95 *Clown.* *[sings]* 'His eyes do show his days are almost done.'

Malvolio. Is't even so?

Toby. *[sings]* 'But I will never die.'

Clown. *[sings]* Sir Toby, there you lie.

Malvolio. This is much credit to you.

100 *Toby.* *[sings]* 'Shall I bid him go?'

Clown. *[sings]* 'What an if you do?'

Toby. *[sings]* 'Shall I bid him go, and spare not?'

Clown. *[sings]* 'O, no, no, no, no, you dare not!'

Toby. Out o' tune, sir? Ye lie. Art any more than a stew-
105 ard? Dost thou think, because thou art virtuous, there
shall be no more cakes and ale?

Clown. Yes, by Saint Anne, and ginger shall be hot i' th'
mouth too.

Toby. Th' art i' th' right. – Go, sir, rub your chain with
110 crumbs. A stoup of wine, Maria!

Malvolio. Mistress Mary, if you prized my lady's favor at
anything more than contempt, you would not give
means for this uncivil rule. She shall know of it, by this
hand.   *Exit.*

115 *Maria.* Go shake your ears.

_____

93 *Farewell, dear heart* . . . (from an old song, 'Corydon's Farewell to
Phyllis') 107 *ginger* (used to spice ale) 109–10 *rub . . . crumbs* (a con-
temptuous allusion to his steward's chain) 112–13 *give means* i.e. bring
the wine 115 *your ears* i.e. your ass's ears

Andrew. 'Twere as good a deed as to drink when a man's ahungry, to challenge him the field, and then to break promise with him and make a fool of him.

Toby. Do't, knight. I'll write thee a challenge; or I'll deliver thy indignation to him by word of mouth.   120

Maria. Sweet Sir Toby, be patient for to-night. Since the youth of the Count's was to-day with my lady, she is much out of quiet. For Monsieur Malvolio, let me alone with him. If I do not gull him into a nayword, and make him a common recreation, do not think I have wit 125 enough to lie straight in my bed. I know I can do it.

Toby. Possess us, possess us. Tell us something of him.

Maria. Marry, sir, sometimes he is a kind of Puritan.

Andrew. O, if I thought that, I'd beat him like a dog.

Toby. What, for being a Puritan? Thy exquisite reason, 130 dear knight.

Andrew. I have no exquisite reason for't, but I have reason good enough.

Maria. The devil a Puritan that he is, or anything constantly but a time-pleaser; an affectioned ass, that cons state with- 135 out book and utters it by great swarths; the best persuaded of himself; so crammed, as he thinks, with excellencies that it is his grounds of faith that all that look on him love him; and on that vice in him will my revenge find notable cause to work.   140

Toby. What wilt thou do?

Maria. I will drop in his way some obscure epistles of love, wherein by the color of his beard, the shape of his leg, the manner of his gait, the expressure of his eye, forehead,

124 *gull* trick *nayword* byword 125 *recreation* amusement 127 *Possess us* give us the facts 135 *time-pleaser* sycophant *affectioned* affected 135-36 *cons . . . book* learns a stately manner by heart 136 *swarths* quantities 144 *expressure* expression

145 and complexion, he shall find himself most feelingly
personated. I can write very like my lady your niece; on a
forgotten matter we can hardly make distinction of our
hands.

Toby. Excellent. I smell a device.

150 *Andrew.* I have't in my nose too.

Toby. He shall think by the letters that thou wilt drop that
they come from my niece, and that she's in love with
him.

Maria. My purpose is indeed a horse of that color.

155 *Andrew.* And your horse now would make him an ass.

Maria. Ass, I doubt not.

Andrew. O, 'twill be admirable.

Maria. Sport royal, I warrant you. I know my physic will
work with him. I will plant you two, and let the fool

160 make a third, where he shall find the letter. Observe his
construction of it. For this night, to bed, and dream on
the event. Farewell.   *Exit.*

Toby. Good night, Penthesilea.

Andrew. Before me, she's a good wench.

165 *Toby.* She's a beagle true-bred, and one that adores me.
What o' that?

Andrew. I was adored once too.

Toby. Let's to bed, knight. Thou hadst need send for more
money.

170 *Andrew.* If I cannot recover your niece, I am a foul way out.

Toby. Send for money, knight. If thou hast her not i' th'
end, call me Cut.

Andrew. If I do not, never trust me, take it how you will.

---

146 *personated* represented   161 *construction* interpretation   162 *event*
outcome   163 *Penthesilea* queen of the Amazons   164 *Before me* I swear by
myself   165 *beagle* small rabbit-hound   170 *recover* gain   *out* out of money
172 *Cut* horse with a docked tail

Toby. Come, come; I'll go burn some sack. 'Tis too late
to go to bed now. Come, knight; come, knight. *Exeunt.* 175

Enter Duke, Viola, Curio, and others.   II, iv

Duke. Give me some music. Now good morrow, friends.
　Now, good Cesario, but that piece of song,
　That old and antique song we heard last night.
　Methought it did relieve my passion much,
　More than light airs and recollected terms   5
　Of these most brisk and giddy-pacèd times.
　Come, but one verse.
Curio. He is not here, so please your lordship, that should
　sing it.
Duke. Who was it?   10
Curio. Feste the jester, my lord, a fool that the Lady Olivia's
　father took much delight in. He is about the house.
Duke. Seek him out, and play the tune the while.
　　　　　　　　　　[Exit Curio.] Music plays.
　Come hither, boy. If ever thou shalt love,
　In the sweet pangs of it remember me;   15
　For such as I am all true lovers are,
　Unstaid and skittish in all motions else
　Save in the constant image of the creature
　That is beloved. How dost thou like this tune?
Viola. It gives a very echo to the seat   20
　Where Love is throned.
Duke.　　　　　　　　Thou dost speak masterly.
　My life upon't, young though thou art, thine eye

174 *burn some sack* warm some sherry II, iv, 3 *antique* quaint 5 *recollected* studied 17 *motions* emotions 20–21 *the seat . . . throned* i.e. the heart

Hath stayed upon some favor that it loves.
Hath it not, boy?

Viola.   A little, by your favor.

Duke. What kind of woman is't?

25 *Viola.*   Of your complexion.

Duke. She is not worth thee then. What years, i' faith?

Viola. About your years, my lord.

Duke. Too old, by heaven. Let still the woman take
    An elder than herself: so wears she to him,
30   So sways she level in her husband's heart;
    For, boy, however we do praise ourselves,
    Our fancies are more giddy and unfirm,
    More longing, wavering, sooner lost and worn,
    Than women's are.

Viola.   I think it well, my lord.

35 *Duke.* Then let thy love be younger than thyself,
    Or thy affection cannot hold the bent;
    For women are as roses, whose fair flow'r,
    Being once displayed, doth fall that very hour.

Viola. And so they are; alas, that they are so.
40   To die, even when they to perfection grow.

Enter Curio and Clown.

Duke. O, fellow, come, the song we had last night.
    Mark it, Cesario; it is old and plain.
    The spinsters and the knitters in the sun,
    And the free maids that weave their thread with bones,
45   Do use to chant it. It is silly sooth,

---

23 *favor* face   29 *wears* adapts herself   30 *sways . . . heart* she keeps constant her husband's love   32 *fancies* loves   36 *bent* direction   43 *spinsters* spinners   44 *free* innocent   *bones* bone bobbins   45 *Do use* are accustomed *silly sooth* simple truth

And dallies with the innocence of love,
    Like the old age.
Clown. Are you ready, sir?
Duke. I prithee sing.   *Music.*

The Song.

Come away, come away, death,   50
    And in sad cypress let me be laid.
Fly away, fly away, breath;
    I am slain by a fair cruel maid.
My shroud of white, stuck all with yew,
    O, prepare it.   55
My part of death, no one so true
    Did share it.

Not a flower, not a flower sweet,
    On my black coffin let there be strown;
Not a friend, not a friend greet   60
    My poor corpse, where my bones shall be
        thrown.
A thousand thousand sighs to save,
    Lay me, O, where
Sad true lover never find my grave,
    To weep there.   65

Duke. There's for thy pains.
Clown. No pains, sir. I take pleasure in singing, sir.
Duke. I'll pay thy pleasure then.
Clown. Truly, sir, and pleasure will be paid one time or
    another.   70
Duke. Give me now leave to leave thee.
Clown. Now the melancholy god protect thee, and the

47 *old age* good old days 51 *cypress* coffin of cypress wood 54 *yew* yew
sprigs, associated with mourning 56 *part* portion 69 *pleasure . . . paid*
indulgence exacts its penalty

tailor make thy doublet of changeable taffeta, for thy
mind is a very opal. I would have men of such constancy
75 put to sea, that their business might be everything, and
their intent everywhere; for that's it that always makes a
good voyage of nothing. Farewell.   *Exit.*

Duke. Let all the rest give place.
                                        [*Exeunt Curio and Attendants.*]
                                        Once more, Cesario,
Get thee to yond same sovereign cruelty.
80 Tell her, my love, more noble than the world,
Prizes not quantity of dirty lands;
The parts that fortune hath bestowed upon her
Tell her I hold as giddily as fortune,
But 'tis that miracle and queen of gems
85 That nature pranks her in attracts my soul.

Viola. But if she cannot love you, sir?

Duke. I cannot be so answered.

Viola.   Sooth, but you must.
Say that some lady, as perhaps there is,
Hath for your love as great a pang of heart
90 As you have for Olivia. You cannot love her.
You tell her so. Must she not then be answered?

Duke. There is no woman's sides
Can bide the beating of so strong a passion
As love doth give my heart; no woman's heart
95 So big to hold so much; they lack retention.
Alas, their love may be called appetite,
No motion of the liver but the palate,
That suffers surfeit, cloyment, and revolt;

73 *changeable* i.e. opalescent in effect   77 *nothing* bringing back nothing
78 *give place* leave   79 *sovereign cruelty* supremely cruel person   82 *parts*
possessions   85 *pranks* decks   93 *bide* withstand   95 *retention* capacity of
retaining   97 *motion* emotion   *liver* seat of the emotion of love   98 *revolt*
revulsion

But mine is all as hungry as the sea
And can digest as much. Make no compare   100
Between that love a woman can bear me
And that I owe Olivia.
Viola.   Ay, but I know.
Duke. What dost thou know?
Viola. Too well what love women to men may owe.
    In faith, they are as true of heart as we.   105
    My father had a daughter loved a man
    As it might be perhaps, were I a woman,
    I should your lordship.
Duke.   And what's her history?
Viola. A blank, my lord. She never told her love,
    But let concealment, like a worm i' th' bud,   110
    Feed on her damask cheek. She pined in thought;
    And, with a green and yellow melancholy,
    She sat like Patience on a monument,
    Smiling at grief. Was not this love indeed?
    We men may say more, swear more; but indeed   115
    Our shows are more than will; for still we prove
    Much in our vows but little in our love.
Duke. But died thy sister of her love, my boy?
Viola. I am all the daughters of my father's house,
    And all the brothers too, and yet I know not.   120
    Sir, shall I to this lady?
Duke.   Ay, that's the theme.
    To her in haste. Give her this jewel. Say
    My love can give no place, bide no denay.   *Exeunt.*

102 *owe* have toward   111 *damask* pink and white, as of a damask rose
116 *will* our passions   123 *can give no place* cannot yield   *denay* denial

II, v   *Enter Sir Toby, Sir Andrew, and Fabian.*

Toby. Come thy ways, Signior Fabian.

Fabian. Nay, I'll come. If I lose a scruple of this sport, let
me be boiled to death with melancholy.

Toby. Wouldst thou not be glad to have the niggardly ras-
5   cally sheep-biter come by some notable shame?

Fabian. I would exult, man. You know he brought me out
o' favor with my lady about a bear-baiting here.

Toby. To anger him we'll have the bear again, and we will
fool him black and blue. Shall we not, Sir Andrew?

10 *Andrew.* An we do not, it is pity of our lives.

Enter Maria.

Toby. Here comes the little villain. How now, my metal of
India?

Maria. Get ye all three into the box tree. Malvolio's coming
down this walk. He has been yonder i' the sun practicing
15   behavior to his own shadow this half hour. Observe him,
for the love of mockery; for I know this letter will make
a contemplative idiot of him. Close, in the name of
jesting. *[The others hide.]* Lie thou there *[throws down a
letter]*; for here comes the trout that must be caught with
20   tickling.   *Exit.*

Enter Malvolio.

Malvolio. 'Tis but fortune; all is fortune. Maria once told
me she did affect me; and I have heard herself come thus

II, v, 2 *scruple* bit   5 *sheep-biter* dog that bites sheep, sneaking fellow
11–12 *my metal of India* my golden one   13 *tree* i.e. hedge   15 *behavior*
elegant conduct   17 *contemplative idiot* i.e. addled by his musings   *Close*
hide   20 *tickling* stroking about the gills   22 *she did affect me* Olivia liked me

near, that, should she fancy, it should be one of my complexion. Besides, she uses me with a more exalted respect
than any one else that follows her. What should I think 25
on't?

Toby. Here's an overweening rogue.

Fabian. O, peace! Contemplation makes a rare turkey cock
of him. How he jets under his advanced plumes!

Andrew. 'Slight, I could so beat the rogue.   30

Toby. Peace, I say.

Malvolio. To be Count Malvolio.

Toby. Ah, rogue!

Andrew. Pistol him, pistol him.

Toby. Peace, peace.   35

Malvolio. There is example for't. The Lady of the Strachy
married the yeoman of the wardrobe.

Andrew. Fie on him, Jezebel.

Fabian. O, peace! Now he's deeply in. Look how imagination blows him.   40

Malvolio. Having been three months married to her, sitting
in my state —

Toby. O for a stone-bow, to hit him in the eye!

Malvolio. Calling my officers about me, in my branched
velvet gown; having come from a day-bed, where I have 45
left Olivia sleeping —

Toby. Fire and brimstone!

Fabian. O, peace, peace!

Malvolio. And then to have the humor of state; and after a
demure travel of regard, telling them I know my place, 50

23-24 *complexion* personality 25 *that follows her* in her service 29 *jets*
struts 30 *'Slight* an oath (by God's light) 36 *Lady of the Strachy* (un-
identified allusion) 38 *Jezebel* wicked queen of Israel 40 *blows him* puffs
him up 42 *state* chair of state 43 *stone-bow* stone-shooter 44 *branched*
embroidered 45 *day-bed* sofa 49 *humor of state* manner and disposition of
authority 50 *demure . . . regard* grave survey

as I would they should do theirs, to ask for my kinsman
Toby —

Toby. Bolts and shackles!

Fabian. O peace, peace, peace, now, now.

55 *Malvolio.* Seven of my people, with an obedient start, make
out for him. I frown the while, and perchance wind up
my watch, or play with my — some rich jewel. Toby ap-
proaches; curtsies there to me —

Toby. Shall this fellow live?

60 *Fabian.* Though our silence be drawn from us with cars,
yet peace.

Malvolio. I extend my hand to him thus, quenching my
familiar smile with an austere regard of control —

Toby. And does not Toby take you a blow o' the lips then?

65 *Malvolio.* Saying, 'Cousin Toby, my fortunes having cast
me on your niece, give me this prerogative of speech.'

Toby. What, what?

Malvolio. 'You must amend your drunkenness.'

Toby. Out, scab!

70 *Fabian.* Nay, patience, or we break the sinews of our plot.

Malvolio. 'Besides, you waste the treasure of your time with
a foolish knight' —

Andrew. That's me, I warrant you.

Malvolio. 'One Sir Andrew' —

75 *Andrew.* I knew 'twas I, for many do call me fool.

Malvolio. What employment have we here?

[Takes up the letter.]

Fabian. Now is the woodcock near the gin.

Toby. O, peace, and the spirit of humors intimate reading
aloud to him!

---

60 *with cars* by force   63 *regard of control* look of authority   64 *take* give
77 *woodcock* (a stupid bird)   *gin* snare, trap

Malvolio. By my life, this is my lady's hand. These be her 80
very C's, her U's, and her T's; and thus makes she her
great P's. It is, in contempt of question, her hand.

Andrew. Her C's, her U's, and her T's? Why that?

Malvolio. [*reads*] 'To the unknown beloved, this, and my
good wishes.' Her very phrases! By your leave, wax. 85
Soft, and the impressure her Lucrece, with which she uses
to seal. 'Tis my lady. To whom should this be?

Fabian. This wins him, liver and all.

Malvolio. [*reads*]

> 'Jove knows I love,
>   But who?
>   Lips, do not move; 90
>   No man must know.'

'No man must know.' What follows? The numbers
altered! 'No man must know.' If this should be thee,
Malvolio? 95

Toby. Marry, hang thee, brock!

Malvolio. [*reads*]

>   'I may command where I adore,
>   But silence, like a Lucrece knife,
>   With bloodless stroke my heart doth gore.
>   M. O. A. I. doth sway my life.' 100

Fabian. A fustian riddle.

Toby. Excellent wench, say I.

Malvolio. 'M. O. A. I. doth sway my life.' Nay, but first, let
me see, let me see, let me see.

Fabian. What dish o' poison has she dressed him! 105

---

82 *in contempt of* beyond 85 *By . . . wax* (a conventional apology for
breaking a seal) 86 *Soft* careful, slow *Lucrece* (her seal was a likeness of the
chaste Lucrece) 88 *liver* the seat of passion 93 *numbers* meter 96 *brock*
badger 101 *fustian* ridiculously lofty 102 *Excellent wench* clever girl
(Maria) 105 *dressed* prepared

Toby. And with what wing the staniel checks at it!

Malvolio. 'I may command where I adore.' Why, she may command me: I serve her; she is my lady. Why, this is evident to any formal capacity. There is no obstruction
110 in this. And the end; what should that alphabetical position portend? If I could make that resemble something in me! Softly, 'M. O. A. I.'

Toby. O, ay, make up that. He is now at a cold scent.

Fabian. Sowter will cry upon't for all this, though it be as
115 rank as a fox.

Malvolio. M. – Malvolio. M. – Why, that begins my name.

Fabian. Did not I say he would work it out? The cur is excellent at faults.

Malvolio. M. – But then there is no consonancy in the
120 sequel. That suffers under probation. A should follow, but O does.

Fabian. And O shall end, I hope.

Toby. Ay, or I'll cudgel him, and make him cry O.

Malvolio. And then I comes behind.

125 *Fabian.* Ay, an you had any eye behind you, you might see more detraction at your heels than fortunes before you.

Malvolio. M, O, A, I. This simulation is not as the former; and yet, to crush this a little, it would bow to me, for every one of these letters are in my name. Soft, here fol-
130 lows prose.

[Reads] 'If this fall into thy hand, revolve. In my stars I am above thee, but be not afraid of greatness. Some are born great, some achieve greatness, and some have great-

---

106 *staniel* an inferior hawk   *checks* turns to pursue the wrong prey   109 *formal* normal   *obstruction* difficulty   113 *cold scent* difficult trail   114 *Sowter . . . upon't* the hound will pick up the scent   118 *faults* gaps or breaks in the scent   119 *consonancy* agreement   120 *suffers* becomes strained   *probation* testing   127 *simulation* hidden meaning   128 *crush* force   131 *revolve* consider   *stars* fate

ness thrust upon 'em. Thy Fates open their hands; let thy
blood and spirit embrace them; and to inure thyself to   135
what thou art like to be, cast thy humble slough and
appear fresh. Be opposite with a kinsman, surly with
servants. Let thy tongue tang arguments of state; put thyself into the trick of singularity. She thus advises thee that
sighs for thee. Remember who commended thy yellow   140
stockings and wished to see thee ever cross-gartered. I
say, remember. Go to, thou art made, if thou desir'st to
be so. If not, let me see thee a steward still, the fellow of
servants, and not worthy to touch Fortune's fingers.
Farewell. She that would alter services with thee,   145
                    'THE FORTUNATE UNHAPPY.'
Daylight and champian discovers not more. This is open.
I will be proud, I will read politic authors, I will baffle Sir
Toby, I will wash off gross acquaintance, I will be point-
devise, the very man. I do not now fool myself, to let   150
imagination jade me, for every reason excites to this, that
my lady loves me. She did commend my yellow stockings of late, she did praise my leg being cross-gartered;
and in this she manifests herself to my love, and with a
kind of injunction drives me to these habits of her liking.   155
I thank my stars, I am happy. I will be strange, stout, in
yellow stockings, and cross-gartered, even with the
swiftness of putting on. Jove and my stars be praised.
Here is yet a postscript.
[Reads] 'Thou canst not choose but know who I am. If   160
thou entertain'st my love, let it appear in thy smiling.

135 *inure* accustom   136 *slough* outer skin   138 *tang* sound with   139
singularity eccentricity   141 *cross-gartered* wearing hose-garters crossed
above and below the knee   146 *Unhappy* unfortunate   147 *champian* open
country   *discovers* reveals, discloses   148 *politic authors* writers on govern-
ment   *baffle* subject to disgrace   149–50 *point-devise* perfectly correct   151
jade trick   155 *habits* attire   156 *strange* aloof   *stout* proud   161 *entertain'st*
accept

71

Thy smiles become thee well. Therefore in my presence
still smile, dear my sweet, I prithee.'

Jove, I thank thee. I will smile; I will do everything that
165 thou wilt have me.   *Exit.*

Fabian. I will not give my part of this sport for a pension of
thousands to be paid from the Sophy.

Toby. I could marry this wench for this device.

Andrew. So could I too.

170 *Toby.* And ask no other dowry with her but such another
jest.

Enter Maria.

Andrew. Nor I neither.

Fabian. Here comes my noble gull-catcher.

Toby. Wilt thou set thy foot o' my neck?

175 *Andrew.* Or o' mine either?

Toby. Shall I play my freedom at tray-trip and become thy
bondslave?

Andrew. I' faith, or I either?

Toby. Why, thou hast put him in such a dream that, when
180 the image of it leaves him, he must run mad.

Maria. Nay, but say true, does it work upon him?

Toby. Like aqua-vitae with a midwife.

Maria. If you will, then, see the fruits of the sport, mark his
first approach before my lady. He will come to her in
185 yellow stockings, and 'tis a color she abhors, and cross-
gartered, a fashion she detests; and he will smile upon her,
which will now be so unsuitable to her disposition, being
addicted to a melancholy as she is, that it cannot but turn
him into a notable contempt. If you will see it, follow me.

167 *Sophy* shah of Persia   173 *gull-catcher* fool-catcher   176 *play* gamble
tray-trip a game of dice   182 *aqua-vitae* any distilled liquor

Toby. To the gates of Tartar, thou most excellent devil of 190
  wit.
Andrew. I'll make one too.   *Exeunt.*

Enter Viola and Clown [with a tabor].   III, i

Viola. Save thee, friend, and thy music. Dost thou live by
  thy tabor?
Clown. No, sir, I live by the church.
Viola. Art thou a churchman?
Clown. No such matter, sir. I do live by the church; for I 5
  do live at my house, and my house doth stand by the
  church.
Viola. So thou mayst say, the king lies by a beggar, if a
  beggar dwell near him; or, the church stands by thy
  tabor, if thy tabor stand by the church.   10
Clown. You have said, sir. To see this age! A sentence is
  but a chev'ril glove to a good wit. How quickly the
  wrong side may be turned outward!
Viola. Nay, that's certain. They that dally nicely with
  words may quickly make them wanton.   15
Clown. I would therefore my sister had had no name, sir.
Viola. Why, man?
Clown. Why, sir, her name's a word, and to dally with that
  word might make my sister wanton. But indeed words
  are very rascals since bonds disgraced them.   20
Viola. Thy reason, man?

190 *Tartar* Tartarus, the section of hell reserved for the most evil III, i, 1
Save thee God save thee *live by* make a living with 2 *tabor* drum 8 *lies*
dwells 12 *chev'ril* kid 14 *dally nicely* play subtly 15 *wanton* capricious
19 *wanton* abandoned 20 *since . . . them* i.e. since bonds have been needed
to guarantee them

Clown. Troth, sir, I can yield you none without words, and
words are grown so false I am loath to prove reason with
them.

25 *Viola.* I warrant thou art a merry fellow and car'st for
nothing.

Clown. Not so, sir; I do care for something; but in my conscience, sir, I do not care for you. If that be to care for
nothing, sir, I would it would make you invisible.

30 *Viola.* Art not thou the Lady Olivia's fool?

Clown. No, indeed, sir. The Lady Olivia has no folly. She
will keep no fool, sir, till she be married; and fools are as
like husbands as pilchers are to herrings, the husband's the
bigger. I am indeed not her fool, but her corrupter of
35 words.

Viola. I saw thee late at the Count Orsino's.

Clown. Foolery, sir, does walk about the orb like the sun;
it shines everywhere. I would be sorry, sir, but the fool
should be as oft with your master as with my mistress. I
40 think I saw your wisdom there.

Viola. Nay, an thou pass upon me, I'll no more with thee.
Hold, there's expenses for thee.   *[Gives a coin.]*

Clown. Now Jove, in his next commodity of hair, send thee
a beard.

45 *Viola.* By my troth, I'll tell thee, I am almost sick for one,
though I would not have it grow on my chin. Is thy lady
within?

Clown. Would not a pair of these have bred, sir?

Viola. Yes, being kept together and put to use.

50 *Clown.* I would play Lord Pandarus of Phrygia, sir, to
bring a Cressida to this Troilus.

---

33 *pilchers* pilchards (small fish resembling herring) 41 *pass upon* jest at
43 *commodity* shipment 49 *put to use* put out at interest 50 *Pandarus* the
go-between in the tale told by Chaucer and others

Viola. I understand you, sir. 'Tis well begged.

                       [Gives another coin.]

Clown. The matter, I hope, is not great, sir, begging but a
    beggar: Cressida was a beggar. My lady is within, sir. I
    will conster to them whence you come. Who you are and   55
    what you would are out of my welkin; I might say 'ele-
    ment,' but the word is over-worn.   *Exit.*

Viola. This fellow is wise enough to play the fool,
    And to do that well craves a kind of wit.
    He must observe their mood on whom he jests,   60
    The quality of persons, and the time;
    Not, like the haggard, check at every feather
    That comes before his eye. This is a practice
    As full of labor as a wise man's art;
    For folly that he wisely shows, is fit;   65
    But wise men, folly-fall'n, quite taint their wit.

        Enter Sir Toby and [Sir] Andrew.

Toby. Save you, gentleman.

Viola. And you, sir.

Andrew. Dieu vous garde, monsieur.

Viola. Et vous aussi; votre serviteur.   70

Andrew. I hope, sir, you are, and I am yours.

Toby. Will you encounter the house? My niece is desirous
    you should enter, if your trade be to her.

Viola. I am bound to your niece, sir; I mean, she is the list
    of my voyage.   75

54 *Cressida was a beggar* (she became a leprous beggar in Henryson's con-
tinuation of Chaucer's story) 55 *conster* construe, explain 56 *welkin* sky
59 *wit* intelligence 62 *haggard* untrained hawk *check . . . feather* forsake
her quarry for other game 63 *practice* skill 66 *folly-fall'n* fallen into folly
taint their wit ruin their reputation for intelligence 69–70 *Dieu . . . serviteur*
God protect you, sir. . . . And you also; your servant 72 *encounter* meet,
i.e. go into 74 *bound to* bound for *list* limit, destination

Toby. Taste your legs, sir; put them to motion.

Viola. My legs do better understand me, sir, than I understand what you mean by bidding me taste my legs.

Toby. I mean, to go, sir, to enter.

80 *Viola.* I will answer you with gait and entrance. But we are prevented.

Enter Olivia and Gentlewoman [Maria].

Most excellent accomplished lady, the heavens rain odors on you.

Andrew. That youth's a rare courtier. 'Rain odors' — well!

85 *Viola.* My matter hath no voice, lady, but to your own most pregnant and vouchsafed ear.

Andrew. 'Odors,' 'pregnant,' and 'vouchsafed' — I'll get 'em all three all ready.

Olivia. Let the garden door be shut, and leave me to my
90 hearing. *[Exeunt Sir Toby, Sir Andrew, and Maria.]* Give me your hand, sir.

Viola. My duty, madam, and most humble service.

Olivia. What is your name?

Viola. Cesario is your servant's name, fair princess.

95 *Olivia.* My servant, sir? 'Twas never merry world
Since lowly feigning was called compliment.
Y' are servant to the Count Orsino, youth.

Viola. And he is yours, and his must needs be yours.
Your servant's servant is your servant, madam.

100 *Olivia.* For him, I think not on him; for his thoughts,
Would they were blanks, rather than filled with me.

Viola. Madam, I come to whet your gentle thoughts
On his behalf.

---

76 *Taste* try   77 *understand* both 'comprehend' and 'stand under'   81 *prevented* anticipated   85 *hath no voice* can be told to no one   86 *pregnant* receptive   96 *lowly feigning* false humility

Olivia.   O, by your leave, I pray you.
  I bade you never speak again of him;
  But, would you undertake another suit,   105
  I had rather hear you to solicit that
  Than music from the spheres.
Viola.   Dear lady —
Olivia. Give me leave, beseech you. I did send,
  After the last enchantment you did here,
  A ring in chase of you. So did I abuse   110
  Myself, my servant, and, I fear me, you.
  Under your hard construction must I sit,
  To force that on you in a shameful cunning
  Which you knew none of yours. What might you think?
  Have you not set mine honor at the stake   115
  And baited it with all th' unmuzzled thoughts
  That tyrannous heart can think? To one of your receiving
  Enough is shown; a cypress, not a bosom,
  Hides my heart. So, let me hear you speak.
Viola. I pity you.
Olivia.   That's a degree to love.   120
Viola. No, not a grize; for 'tis a vulgar proof
  That very oft we pity enemies.
Olivia. Why then, methinks 'tis time to smile again.
  O world, how apt the poor are to be proud.
  If one should be a prey, how much the better   125
  To fall before the lion than the wolf.   *Clock strikes.*
  The clock upbraids me with the waste of time.
  Be not afraid, good youth, I will not have you,
  And yet, when wit and youth is come to harvest,

107 *spheres* the several concentric revolving spheres in which the planets and stars were thought to be placed 110 *abuse* deceive 112 *construction* interpretation 116 *baited* harassed, as a bear by dogs 117 *receiving* receptive capacity 118 *cypress* transparent black cloth 121 *grize* grece, flight of steps *vulgar proof* common experience

77

130 Your wife is like to reap a proper man.
There lies your way, due west.

Viola.   Then westward ho!
Grace and good disposition attend your ladyship.
You'll nothing, madam, to my lord by me?

Olivia. Stay.
135 I prithee tell me what thou think'st of me.

Viola. That you do think you are not what you are.

Olivia. If I think so, I think the same of you.

Viola. Then think you right. I am not what I am.

Olivia. I would you were as I would have you be.

140 *Viola.* Would it be better, madam, than I am?
I wish it might, for now I am your fool.

Olivia. O, what a deal of scorn looks beautiful
In the contempt and anger of his lip.
A murd'rous guilt shows not itself more soon
145 Than love that would seem hid: love's night is noon.
Cesario, by the roses of the spring,
By maidhood, honor, truth, and everything,
I love thee so that, maugre all thy pride,
Nor wit nor reason can my passion hide.
150 Do not extort thy reasons from this clause,
For that I woo, thou therefore hast no cause;
But rather reason thus with reason fetter,
Love sought is good, but given unsought is better.

Viola. By innocence I swear, and by my youth,
155 I have one heart, one bosom, and one truth,
And that no woman has; nor never none
Shall mistress be of it, save I alone.
And so adieu, good madam. Never more
Will I my master's tears to you deplore.

130 *proper* handsome   141 *fool* butt   148 *maugre* despite

Olivia. Yet come again; for thou perhaps mayst move   160
That heart which now abhors to like his love.   *Exeunt.*

Enter Sir Toby, Sir Andrew, and Fabian.   III, ii

Andrew. No, faith, I'll not stay a jot longer.

Toby. Thy reason, dear venom; give thy reason.

Fabian. You must needs yield your reason, Sir Andrew.

Andrew. Marry, I saw your niece do more favors to the Count's servingman than ever she bestowed upon me. I 5 saw't i' th' orchard.

Toby. Did she see thee the while, old boy? Tell me that.

Andrew. As plain as I see you now.

Fabian. This was a great argument of love in her toward you.   10

Andrew. 'Slight! will you make an ass o' me?

Fabian. I will prove it legitimate, sir, upon the oaths of judgment and reason.

Toby. And they have been grand-jurymen since before Noah was a sailor.   15

Fabian. She did show favor to the youth in your sight only to exasperate you, to awake your dormouse valor, to put fire in your heart and brimstone in your liver. You should then have accosted her, and with some excellent jests, fire-new from the mint, you should have banged the 20 youth into dumbness. This was looked for at your hand, and this was balked. The double gilt of this opportunity you let time wash off, and you are now sailed

III, ii, 6 *orchard* probably 'garden'   9 *argument* proof   12 *legitimate* true *oaths* testimony   17 *dormouse* i.e. sleepy   22 *balked* missed

into the North of my lady's opinion, where you will hang
25   like an icicle on a Dutchman's beard unless you do redeem
it by some laudable attempt either of valor or policy.

Andrew. An't be any way, it must be with valor; for policy
I hate. I had as lief be a Brownist as a politician.

Toby. Why then, build me thy fortunes upon the basis of
30   valor. Challenge me the Count's youth to fight with him;
hurt him in eleven places. My niece shall take note of it,
and assure thyself there is no love-broker in the world can
more prevail in man's commendation with woman than
report of valor.

35   *Fabian.* There is no way but this, Sir Andrew.

Andrew. Will either of you bear me a challenge to him?

Toby. Go, write it in a martial hand. Be curst and brief; it
is no matter how witty, so it be eloquent and full of invention. Taunt him with the license of ink. If thou thou'st
40   him some thrice, it shall not be amiss; and as many lies as
will lie in thy sheet of paper, although the sheet were big
enough for the bed of Ware in England, set 'em down.
Go about it. Let there be gall enough in thy ink, though
thou write with a goose-pen, no matter. About it!

45   *Andrew.* Where shall I find you?

Toby. We'll call thee at the cubiculo. Go.

Exit Sir Andrew.

Fabian. This is a dear manikin to you, Sir Toby.

Toby. I have been dear to him, lad, some two thousand
strong or so.

50   *Fabian.* We shall have a rare letter from him, but you'll not
deliver't?

24 *into the North* i.e. out of the warmth 28 *Brownist* early Congrega-
tionalist 37 *curst* perversely cross 39 *license of ink* i.e. unrestrained writing
39–40 *thou'st him* call him 'thou' instead of the polite 'you' 42 *bed of Ware*
a famous bed, over ten feet wide 46 *cubiculo* little chamber 47 *manikin*
puppet

Toby. Never trust me then; and by all means stir on the youth to an answer. I think oxen and wainropes cannot hale them together. For Andrew, if he were opened, and you find so much blood in his liver as will clog the foot of 55 a flea, I'll eat the rest of th' anatomy.

Fabian. And his opposite, the youth, bears in his visage no great presage of cruelty.

Enter Maria.

Toby. Look where the youngest wren of mine comes.

Maria. If you desire the spleen, and will laugh yourselves 60 into stitches, follow me. Yond gull Malvolio is turned heathen, a very renegado; for there is no Christian that means to be saved by believing rightly can ever believe such impossible passages of grossness. He's in yellow stockings. 65

Toby. And cross-gartered?

Maria. Most villainously; like a pedant that keeps a school i' th' church. I have dogged him like his murderer. He does obey every point of the letter that I dropped to betray him. He does smile his face into more lines than is in 70 the new map with the augmentation of the Indies. You have not seen such a thing as 'tis. I can hardly forbear hurling things at him. I know my lady will strike him. If she do, he'll smile, and take't for a great favor.

Toby. Come bring us, bring us where he is. 75

Exeunt omnes.

53 *wainropes* wagon ropes   54 *hale* haul   59 *youngest wren* smallest of small birds   60 *spleen* a laughing fit   61 *gull* dupe   64 *passages of grossness* statements of exaggerated misinformation   71 *map . . . Indies* (Emerie Molyneux's map, c. 1599, which gave fuller details of the East Indies and North America, with meridian lines, etc.)

Enter Sebastian and Antonio.

Sebastian. I would not by my will have troubled you;
  But since you make your pleasure of your pains,
  I will no further chide you.
Antonio. I could not stay behind you. My desire
5 (More sharp than filèd steel) did spur me forth;
  And not all love to see you (though so much
  As might have drawn one to a longer voyage)
  But jealousy what might befall your travel,
  Being skilless in these parts; which to a stranger,
10 Unguided and unfriended, often prove
  Rough and unhospitable. My willing love,
  The rather by these arguments of fear,
  Set forth in your pursuit.
Sebastian.   My kind Antonio,
  I can no other answer make but thanks,
15 And thanks, and ever oft good turns
  Are shuffled off with such uncurrent pay.
  But, were my worth as is my conscience firm,
  You should find better dealing. What's to do?
  Shall we go see the relics of this town?
20 *Antonio.* To-morrow, sir; best first go see your lodging.
Sebastian. I am not weary, and 'tis long to night.
  I pray you let us satisfy our eyes
  With the memorials and the things of fame
  That do renown this city.
Antonio.   Would you'ld pardon me.
25 I do not without danger walk these streets.
  Once in a sea-fight 'gainst the Count his galleys

III, iii, 6 *not all* not only, not entirely 8 *jealousy* solicitude 9 *skilless in* without knowledge of 16 *uncurrent* valueless 17 *worth* wealth *conscience* right inclination 19 *relics* monuments

I did some service; of such note indeed
That, were I ta'en here, it would scarce be answered.

Sebastian. Belike you slew great number of his people?

Antonio. Th' offense is not of such a bloody nature, 30
Albeit the quality of the time and quarrel
Might well have given us bloody argument.
It might have since been answered in repaying
What we took from them, which for traffic's sake
Most of our city did. Only myself stood out; 35
For which, if I be lapsèd in this place,
I shall pay dear.

Sebastian. Do not then walk too open.

Antonio. It doth not fit me. Hold, sir, here's my purse.
In the south suburbs at the Elephant
Is best to lodge. I will bespeak our diet, 40
Whiles you beguile the time and feed your knowledge
With viewing of the town. There shall you have me.

Sebastian. Why I your purse?

Antonio. Haply your eye shall light upon some toy
You have desire to purchase, and your store 45
I think is not for idle markets, sir.

Sebastian. I'll be your purse-bearer, and leave you for
An hour.

Antonio. To th' Elephant.

Sebastian. I do remember. *Exeunt.*

28 *answered* atoned for 34 *traffic's* trade's 36 *lapsèd* surprised, pounced upon 39 *the Elephant* an inn 44 *toy* trifle 45 *store* store of money 46 *idle markets* useless purchasings

III, iv   *Enter Olivia and Maria.*

Olivia. I have sent after him; he says he'll come.
How shall I feast him? What bestow of him?
For youth is bought more oft than begged or borrowed.
I speak too loud. Where's Malvolio? He is sad and civil,
5   And suits well for a servant with my fortunes.
Where is Malvolio?

Maria. He's coming, madam, but in very strange manner.
He is sure possessed, madam.

Olivia. Why, what's the matter? Does he rave?

10 *Maria.* No, madam, he does nothing but smile. Your ladyship were best to have some guard about you if he come,
for sure the man is tainted in 's wits.

Olivia. Go call him hither. I am as mad as he,
If sad and merry madness equal be.

Enter Malvolio.

15   How now, Malvolio?

Malvolio. Sweet lady, ho, ho!

Olivia. Smil'st thou? I sent for thee upon a sad occasion.

Malvolio. Sad, lady? I could be sad. This does make some
obstruction in the blood, this cross-gartering; but what
20   of that? If it please the eye of one, it is with me as the very
true sonnet is, 'Please one, and please all.'

Olivia. Why, how dost thou, man? What is the matter with
thee?

Malvolio. Not black in my mind, though yellow in my
25   legs. It did come to his hands, and commands shall be
executed. I think we do know the sweet Roman hand.

III, iv, 4 *sad and civil* serious and sedate 8 *possessed* mad 21 *sonnet* any
short poem 26 *Roman hand* Italian style of handwriting

Olivia. Wilt thou go to bed, Malvolio?

Malvolio. To bed? Ay, sweetheart, and I'll come to thee.

Olivia. God comfort thee. Why dost thou smile so, and kiss thy hand so oft? 30

Maria. How do you, Malvolio?

Malvolio. At your request? Yes, nightingales answer daws!

Maria. Why appear you with this ridiculous boldness before my lady?

Malvolio. 'Be not afraid of greatness.' 'Twas well writ. 35

Olivia. What mean'st thou by that, Malvolio?

Malvolio. 'Some are born great.'

Olivia. Ha?

Malvolio. 'Some achieve greatness.'

Olivia. What say'st thou? 40

Malvolio. 'And some have greatness thrust upon them.'

Olivia. Heaven restore thee!

Malvolio. 'Remember who commended thy yellow stockings.'

Olivia. Thy yellow stockings? 45

Malvolio. 'And wished to see thee cross-gartered.'

Olivia. Cross-gartered?

Malvolio. 'Go to, thou art made, if thou desir'st to be so.'

Olivia. Am I made?

Malvolio. 'If not, let me see thee a servant still.' 50

Olivia. Why, this is very midsummer madness.

Enter Servant.

Servant. Madam, the young gentleman of the Count Orsino's is returned. I could hardly entreat him back. He attends your ladyship's pleasure.

Olivia. I'll come to him. *[Exit Servant.]* Good Maria, let 55 this fellow be looked to. Where's my cousin Toby? Let

some of my people have a special care of him. I would
not have him miscarry for the half of my dowry.

Exit [Olivia; then Maria].

Malvolio. O ho, do you come near me now? No worse man
60 than Sir Toby to look to me. This concurs directly with
the letter. She sends him on purpose, that I may appear
stubborn to him; for she incites me to that in the letter.
'Cast thy humble slough,' says she; 'be opposite with a
kinsman, surly with servants; let thy tongue tang with
65 arguments of state; put thyself into the trick of singularity.' And consequently sets down the manner how: as,
a sad face, a reverend carriage, a slow tongue, in the
habit of some sir of note, and so forth. I have limed her;
but it is Jove's doing, and Jove make me thankful. And
70 when she went away now, 'Let this fellow be looked to.'
'Fellow.' Not 'Malvolio,' nor after my degree, but 'fellow.' Why, everything adheres together, that no dram of
a scruple, no scruple of a scruple, no obstacle, no incredulous or unsafe circumstance – what can be said? Nothing
75 that can be can come between me and the full prospect of
my hopes. Well, Jove, not I, is the doer of this, and he is
to be thanked.

Enter [Sir] Toby, Fabian, and Maria.

Toby. Which way is he, in the name of sanctity? If all the
devils of hell be drawn in little, and Legion himself pos-
80 sessed him, yet I'll speak to him.
Fabian. Here he is, here he is! How is't with you, sir?

58 *miscarry* come to harm 62 *stubborn* hard, stiff, rigid 68 *limed* caught
71 *Fellow* companion *after my degree* according to my position 72 *dram*
(1) small bit (2) one-eighth fluid ounce 73 *scruple* (1) doubt (2) one-third
of a dram 73–74 *incredulous* incredible 79 *drawn in little* brought together
in a small space *Legion* troop of fiends

Toby. How is't with you, man?

Malvolio. Go off; I discard you. Let me enjoy my private. Go off.

Maria. Lo, how hollow the fiend speaks within him! Did 85 not I tell you? Sir Toby, my lady prays you to have a care of him.

Malvolio. Aha! does she so?

Toby. Go to, go to; peace, peace; we must deal gently with him. Let me alone. How do you, Malvolio? How is't 90 with you? What, man, defy the devil? Consider, he's an enemy to mankind.

Malvolio. Do you know what you say?

Maria. La you, an you speak ill of the devil, how he takes it at heart. Pray God he be not bewitched. 95

Fabian. Carry his water to th' wise woman.

Maria. Marry, and it shall be done to-morrow morning if I live. My lady would not lose him for more than I'll say.

Malvolio. How now, mistress?

Maria. O Lord. 100

Toby. Prithee hold thy peace. This is not the way. Do you not see you move him? Let me alone with him.

Fabian. No way but gentleness; gently, gently. The fiend is rough and will not be roughly used.

Toby. Why, how now, my bawcock? How dost thou, 105 chuck?

Malvolio. Sir.

Toby. Ay, biddy, come with me. What, man, 'tis not for gravity to play at cherry-pit with Satan. Hang him, foul collier! 110

96 *wise woman* herb woman 102 *move* rouse 105 *bawcock* fine fellow (French *beau coq*) 106 *chuck* chick 108 *biddy* chicken 109 *gravity* dignity *cherry-pit* a child's game 110 *collier* coal peddler

Maria. Get him to say his prayers; good Sir Toby, get him
to pray.

Malvolio. My prayers, minx?

Maria. No, I warrant you, he will not hear of godliness.

115 *Malvolio.* Go hang yourselves all! You are idle shallow
things; I am not of your element. You shall know more
hereafter.   *Exit.*

Toby. Is't possible?

Fabian. If this were played upon a stage now, I could con-
120 demn it as an improbable fiction.

Toby. His very genius hath taken the infection of the device, man.

Maria. Nay, pursue him now, lest the device take air and
taint.

125 *Fabian.* Why, we shall make him mad indeed.

Maria. The house will be the quieter.

Toby. Come, we'll have him in a dark room and bound.
My niece is already in the belief that he's mad. We may
carry it thus, for our pleasure and his penance, till our
130 very pastime, tired out of breath, prompt us to have
mercy on him; at which time we will bring the device to
the bar and crown thee for a finder of madmen. But see,
but see.

Enter Sir Andrew.

Fabian. More matter for a May morning.

135 *Andrew.* Here's the challenge; read it. I warrant there's
vinegar and pepper in't.

Fabian. Is't so saucy?

Andrew. Ay, is't, I warrant him. Do but read.

---

115 *idle* empty, trifling   121 *genius* nature   123–24 *take air and taint* be
exposed and thus contaminated   129 *carry it* carry the trick on   134 *matter
. . . morning* material for a May-day comedy   137 *saucy* (1) spicy (2) impudent, sharp

Toby. Give me. *[reads]* 'Youth, whatsoever thou art, thou
   art but a scurvy fellow.'   140

Fabian. Good, and valiant.

Toby. *[reads]* 'Wonder not nor admire not in thy mind
   why I do call thee so, for I will show thee no reason for't.'

Fabian. A good note that keeps you from the blow of the
   law.   145

Toby. *[reads]* 'Thou com'st to the Lady Olivia, and in my
   sight she uses thee kindly. But thou liest in thy throat;
   that is not the matter I challenge thee for.'

Fabian. Very brief, and to exceeding good sense – less.

Toby. *[reads]* 'I will waylay thee going home; where if it   150
   be thy chance to kill me' –

Fabian. Good.

Toby. *[reads]* 'Thou kill'st me like a rogue and a villain.'

Fabian. Still you keep o' th' windy side of the law. Good.

Toby. *[reads]* 'Fare thee well, and God have mercy upon   155
   one of our souls. He may have mercy upon mine, but my
   hope is better, and so look to thyself. Thy friend, as thou
   usest him, and thy sworn enemy,

                                   'ANDREW AGUECHEEK.'

   If this letter move him not, his legs cannot. I'll give't him. 160

Maria. You may have very fit occasion for't. He is now in
   some commerce with my lady and will by and by depart.

Toby. Go, Sir Andrew. Scout me for him at the corner of
   the orchard like a bum-baily. So soon as ever thou seest
   him, draw; and as thou draw'st, swear horrible; for it   165
   comes to pass oft that a terrible oath, with a swaggering
   accent sharply twanged off, gives manhood more approbation than ever proof itself would have earned him.
   Away!

---

154 *windy* windward, safe   164 *bum-baily* an agent employed in making
arrests   167–68 *manhood more approbation* more reputation for courage
168 *proof* testing

170 *Andrew.* Nay, let me alone for swearing.   *[Exit.]*
    Toby. Now will not I deliver his letter; for the behavior of
the young gentleman gives him out to be of good capacity and breeding; his employment between his lord and
my niece confirms no less. Therefore this letter, being so
175 excellently ignorant, will breed no terror in the youth.
He will find it comes from a clodpoll. But, sir, I will deliver his challenge by word of mouth, set upon Aguecheek a notable report of valor, and drive the gentleman
(as I know his youth will aptly receive it) into a most
180 hideous opinion of his rage, skill, fury, and impetuosity.
This will so fright them both that they will kill one
another by the look, like cockatrices.

Enter Olivia and Viola.

    Fabian. Here he comes with your niece. Give them way till
he take leave, and presently after him.
185 *Toby.* I will meditate the while upon some horrid message
for a challenge.   *[Exeunt Sir Toby, Fabian, and Maria.]*
    Olivia. I have said too much unto a heart of stone
And laid mine honor too unchary on't.
There's something in me that reproves my fault;
190 But such a headstrong potent fault it is
That it but mocks reproof.
    Viola. With the same havior that your passion bears
Goes on my master's griefs.
    Olivia. Here, wear this jewel for me; 'tis my picture.
195 Refuse it not; it hath no tongue to vex you.
And I beseech you come again to-morrow.

170 *let . . . swearing* leave swearing to me 182 *cockatrices* basilisks, reptiles
able to kill with a glance 188 *unchary on't* carelessly on it (the heart of
stone) 192 *havior* behavior 194 *jewel* any ornament or trinket; here
perhaps 'locket'

What shall you ask of me that I'll deny,
That honor, saved, may upon asking give?
Viola. Nothing but this: your true love for my master.
Olivia. How with mine honor may I give him that   200
Which I have given to you?
Viola.   I will acquit you.
Olivia. Well, come again to-morrow. Fare thee well.
A fiend like thee might bear my soul to hell.   *[Exit.]*

Enter [Sir] Toby and Fabian.

Toby. Gentleman, God save thee.
Viola. And you, sir.   205
Toby. That defense thou hast, betake thee to't. Of what
nature the wrongs are thou hast done him, I know not;
but thy intercepter, full of despite, bloody as the hunter,
attends thee at the orchard end. Dismount thy tuck, be
yare in thy preparation, for thy assailant is quick, skillful,   210
and deadly.
Viola. You mistake, sir. I am sure no man hath any quarrel
to me. My remembrance is very free and clear from any
image of offense done to any man.
Toby. You'll find it otherwise, I assure you. Therefore, if   215
you hold your life at any price, betake you to your guard;
for your opposite hath in him what youth, strength, skill,
and wrath can furnish man withal.
Viola. I pray you, sir, what is he?
Toby. He is knight, dubbed with unhatched rapier and on   220
carpet consideration, but he is a devil in private brawl.
Souls and bodies hath he divorced three; and his incense-

203 *like thee* in your likeness 208 *despite* defiance 209 *Dismount thy tuck*
take out your rapier 210 *yare* quick 220 *unhatched* unhacked 220-21 *on
carpet consideration* through court favor

ment at this moment is so implacable that satisfaction can
be none but by pangs of death and sepulchre. 'Hob, nob'
225　is his word; 'give't or take't.'

Viola. I will return again into the house and desire some
conduct of the lady. I am no fighter. I have heard of some
kind of men that put quarrels purposely on others to
taste their valor. Belike this is a man of that quirk.

230　*Toby.* Sir, no. His indignation derives itself out of a very
competent injury; therefore get you on and give him his
desire. Back you shall not to the house, unless you undertake that with me which with as much safety you might
answer him. Therefore on, or strip your sword stark
235　naked; for meddle you must, that's certain, or forswear
to wear iron about you.

Viola. This is as uncivil as strange. I beseech you do me this
courteous office, as to know of the knight what my
offense to him is. It is something of my negligence, noth-
240　ing of my purpose.

Toby. I will do so. Signior Fabian, stay you by this gentleman till my return.   *Exit.*

Viola. Pray you, sir, do you know of this matter?

Fabian. I know the knight is incensed against you, even to a
245　mortal arbitrement; but nothing of the circumstance
more.

Viola. I beseech you, what manner of man is he?

Fabian. Nothing of that wonderful promise, to read him by
his form, as you are like to find him in the proof of his
250　valor. He is indeed, sir, the most skillful, bloody, and fatal
opposite that you could possibly have found in any part

---

224 *Hob, nob* have or have not   227 *conduct* protective escort   229 *taste*
test   *quirk* peculiarity   231 *competent* sufficient   235 *meddle* engage (in the
fight)   235–36 *forswear . . . iron* repudiate on oath (your right) to wear a
sword   245 *mortal arbitrement* deadly settlement

of Illyria. Will you walk towards him? I will make your
peace with him if I can.

Viola. I shall be much bound to you for't. I am one that had
rather go with sir priest than sir knight. I care not who   255
knows so much of my mettle.   *Exeunt.*

Enter [Sir] Toby and [Sir] Andrew.

Toby. Why, man, he's a very devil; I have not seen such a
firago. I had a pass with him, rapier, scabbard, and all,
and he gives me the stuck-in with such a mortal motion
that it is inevitable; and on the answer he pays you as   260
surely as your feet hits the ground they step on. They say
he has been fencer to the Sophy.

Andrew. Pox on't, I'll not meddle with him.

Toby. Ay, but he will not now be pacified. Fabian can
scarce hold him yonder.   265

Andrew. Plague on't, an I thought he had been valiant, and
so cunning in fence, I'd have seen him damned ere I'd
have challenged him. Let him let the matter slip, and I'll
give him my horse, grey Capilet.

Toby. I'll make the motion. Stand here; make a good show   270
on't. This shall end without the perdition of souls.
[aside] Marry, I'll ride your horse as well as I ride you.

Enter Fabian and Viola.

I have his horse to take up the quarrel. I have persuaded
him the youth's a devil.

Fabian. He is as horribly conceited of him, and pants and   275
looks pale, as if a bear were at his heels.

258 *firago* virago *pass* bout   259 *stuck-in* thrust, lunge *motion* offer   260
answer return   270 *motion* offer   271 *the perdition of souls* i.e. killing   273
take up settle   275 *He . . . him* he (Cesario) has just as frightening a con-
ception of him (Sir Andrew)

Toby. There's no remedy, sir; he will fight with you for 's
oath sake. Marry, he hath better bethought him of his
quarrel, and he finds that now scarce to be worth talking
280 of. Therefore draw for the supportance of his vow. He
protests he will not hurt you.

Viola. [aside] Pray God defend me! A little thing would
make me tell them how much I lack of a man.

Fabian. Give ground if you see him furious.

285 *Toby.* Come, Sir Andrew, there's no remedy. The gentleman will for his honor's sake have one bout with you; he
cannot by the duello avoid it; but he has promised me,
as he is a gentleman and a soldier, he will not hurt you.
Come on, to't.

290 *Andrew.* Pray God he keep his oath!   *[Draws.]*

Enter Antonio.

Viola. I do assure you 'tis against my will.   *[Draws.]*

Antonio. Put up your sword. If this young gentleman
Have done offense, I take the fault on me;
If you offend him, I for him defy you.

295 *Toby.* You, sir? Why, what are you?

Antonio. [draws] One, sir, that for his love dares yet do more
Than you have heard him brag to you he will.

Toby. Nay, if you be an undertaker, I am for you. *[Draws.]*

Enter Officers.

Fabian. O good Sir Toby, hold. Here come the officers.

300 *Toby. [to Antonio]* I'll be with you anon.

Viola. [to Sir Andrew] Pray, sir, put your sword up, if you
please.

Andrew. Marry, will I, sir; and for that I promised you,

287 *duello* duelling code   298 *undertaker* one who takes up a challenge

I'll be as good as my word. He will bear you easily, and
reins well.   305

1. Officer. This is the man; do thy office.

2. Officer. Antonio, I arrest thee at the suit
Of Count Orsino.

Antonio.   You do mistake me, sir.

1. Officer. No, sir, no jot. I know your favor well,
Though now you have no sea-cap on your head.   310
Take him away. He knows I know him well.

Antonio. I must obey. *[to Viola]* This comes with seeking
  you.
But there's no remedy; I shall answer it.
What will you do, now my necessity
Makes me to ask you for my purse? It grieves me 315
Much more for what I cannot do for you
Than what befalls myself. You stand amazed,
But be of comfort.

2. Officer. Come, sir, away.

Antonio. I must entreat of you some of that money. 320

Viola. What money, sir?
For the fair kindness you have showed me here,
And part being prompted by your present trouble,
Out of my lean and low ability
I'll lend you something. My having is not much.   325
I'll make division of my present with you.
Hold, there's half my coffer.

Antonio.   Will you deny me now?
Is't possible that my deserts to you
Can lack persuasion? Do not tempt my misery,
Lest that it make me so unsound a man   330
As to upbraid you with those kindnesses
That I have done for you.

309 *favor* face   326 *my present* what I have now   327 *coffer* money

95

Viola.   I know of none,
Nor know I you by voice or any feature.
I hate ingratitude more in a man
335 Than lying, vainness, babbling, drunkenness,
Or any taint of vice whose strong corruption
Inhabits our frail blood.

Antonio.   O heavens themselves!

2. Officer. Come, sir, I pray you go.

Antonio. Let me speak a little. This youth that you see here
340 I snatched one half out of the jaws of death;
Relieved him with such sanctity of love,
And to his image, which methought did promise
Most venerable worth, did I devotion.

1. Officer. What's that to us? The time goes by. Away.

345 *Antonio.* But, O, how vile an idol proves this god!
Thou hast, Sebastian, done good feature shame.
In nature there's no blemish but the mind;
None can be called deformed but the unkind.
Virtue is beauty; but the beauteous evil
350 Are empty trunks, o'erflourished by the devil.

1. Officer. The man grows mad; away with him! Come,
come, sir.

Antonio. Lead me on.   *Exit [with Officers].*

Viola. Methinks his words do from such passion fly
That he believes himself; so do not I.
355 Prove true, imagination, O, prove true,
That I, dear brother, be now ta'en for you!

Toby. Come hither, knight; come hither, Fabian. We'll
whisper o'er a couplet or two of most sage saws.

Viola. He named Sebastian. I my brother know

---

343 *venerable* worthy of veneration   348 *unkind* unnatural   349 *beauteous*
fair-seeming   350 *trunks* chests   *o'erflourished* ornamented   358 *sage saws*
wise sayings

Yet living in my glass. Even such and so   360
In favor was my brother, and he went
Still in this fashion, color, ornament,
For him I imitate. O, if it prove,
Tempests are kind, and salt waves fresh in love! *[Exit.]*

Toby. A very dishonest paltry boy, and more a coward 365
than a hare. His dishonesty appears in leaving his friend
here in necessity and denying him; and for his coward-
ship, ask Fabian.

Fabian. A coward, a most devout coward; religious in it.

Andrew. 'Slid, I'll after him again and beat him.   370

Toby. Do; cuff him soundly, but never draw thy sword.

Andrew. An I do not —   *[Exit.]*

Fabian. Come, let's see the event.

Toby. I dare lay any money 'twill be nothing yet. *Exeunt.*

Enter Sebastian and Clown.   IV, i

Clown. Will you make me believe that I am not sent for
you?

Sebastian. Go to, go to, thou art a foolish fellow. Let me be
clear of thee.

Clown. Well held out, i' faith! No, I do not know you; 5
nor I am not sent to you by my lady, to bid you come
speak with her; nor your name is not Master Cesario;
nor this is not my nose neither. Nothing that is so is so.

Sebastian. I prithee vent thy folly somewhere else. Thou
know'st not me.   10

---

360 *Yet . . . glass* i.e. whenever I look in the mirror   365 *dishonest* dishonorable   369 *religious* confirmed   373 *event* result   374 *yet* nevertheless
IV, i, 5 *held out* kept up

97

Clown. Vent my folly! He has heard that word of some
great man, and now applies it to a fool. Vent my folly!
I am afraid this great lubber, the world, will prove a
cockney. I prithee now, ungird thy strangeness, and tell
15 me what I shall vent to my lady. Shall I vent to her that
thou art coming?

Sebastian. I prithee, foolish Greek, depart from me. There's
money for thee. If you tarry longer, I shall give worse
payment.

20 *Clown.* By my troth, thou hast an open hand. These wise
men that give fools money get themselves a good report
— after fourteen years' purchase.

Enter [Sir] Andrew, [Sir] Toby, and Fabian.

Andrew. Now, sir, have I met you again? There's for you!
                                        [*Strikes Sebastian.*]
Sebastian. Why, there's for thee, and there, and there!
                                        [*Strikes Sir Andrew.*]
25 Are all the people mad?

Toby. Hold, sir, or I'll throw your dagger o'er the house.
                                        [*Seizes Sebastian.*]
Clown. This will I tell my lady straight. I would not be in
some of your coats for two-pence.   *Exit.*

Toby. Come on, sir; hold.

30 *Andrew.* Nay, let him alone. I'll go another way to work
with him. I'll have an action of battery against him, if
there be any law in Illyria. Though I struck him first, yet
it's no matter for that.

Sebastian. Let go thy hand.

13 *lubber* lout 14 *cockney* affected person *ungird thy strangeness* abandon
your strange manner 17 *Greek* merry companion 22 *after . . . purchase* i.e.
at a high price 31 *action of battery* suit at law for beating (me)

Toby. Come, sir, I will not let you go. Come, my young 35
  soldier, put up your iron. You are well fleshed. Come on.
Sebastian. I will be free from thee. *[Frees himself.]* What
  wouldst thou now?
  If thou dar'st tempt me further, draw thy sword. *[Draws.]*
Toby. What, what? Nay then, I must have an ounce or two
  of this malapert blood from you. *[Draws.]* 40

Enter Olivia.

Olivia. Hold, Toby! On thy life I charge thee hold!
Toby. Madam.
Olivia. Will it be ever thus? Ungracious wretch,
  Fit for the mountains and the barbarous caves,
  Where manners ne'er were preached! Out of my sight! 45
  Be not offended, dear Cesario.
  Rudesby, be gone.
            [Exeunt Sir Toby, Sir Andrew, and Fabian.]
                       I prithee, gentle friend,
  Let thy fair wisdom, not thy passion, sway
  In this uncivil and unjust extent
  Against thy peace. Go with me to my house, 50
  And hear thou there how many fruitless pranks
  This ruffian hath botched up, that thou thereby
  Mayst smile at this. Thou shalt not choose but go.
  Do not deny. Beshrew his soul for me.
  He started one poor heart of mine, in thee. 55
Sebastian. What relish is in this? How runs the stream?
  Or I am mad, or else this is a dream.

36 *well fleshed* made fierce by a taste of blood   40 *malapert* impudent
47 *Rudesby* unmannerly fellow   49 *uncivil* uncivilized   *extent* probably
'display'   52 *botched up* contrived   54 *Beshrew* curse   55 *started* startled
heart (with a pun on *hart*)   56 *relish* taste

Let fancy still my sense in Lethe steep;
If it be thus to dream, still let me sleep!
Olivia. Nay, come, I prithee. Would thou'dst be ruled by
60 me!
Sebastian. Madam, I will.
Olivia.   O, say so, and so be.   *Exeunt.*

IV, ii   *Enter Maria and Clown.*

Maria. Nay, I prithee put on this gown and this beard;
make him believe thou art Sir Topas the curate; do it
quickly. I'll call Sir Toby the whilst.   *[Exit.]*
Clown. Well, I'll put it on, and I will dissemble myself in't,
5 and I would I were the first that ever dissembled in such a
gown. I am not tall enough to become the function well,
nor lean enough to be thought a good student; but to be
said an honest man and a good housekeeper goes as
fairly as to say a careful man and a great scholar. The
10 competitors enter.

           Enter [Sir] Toby [and Maria].

Toby. Jove bless thee, Master Parson.
Clown. Bonos dies, Sir Toby; for, as the old hermit of
Prague, that never saw pen and ink, very wittily said to a
niece of King Gorboduc, 'That that is is'; so, I, being

58 *Lethe* the river of forgetfulness in the underworld IV, ii, 2 *Sir* (common title of address for the clergy) *Topas* (comic knight in Chaucer; the topaz stone was thought to cure insanity) 4 *dissemble* disguise 6 *function* function of a cleric 8 *good housekeeper* householder, neighbor 10 *competitors* associates 12 *Bonos dies* good day 12–13 *the old hermit of Prague* (probably the clown's invention) 14 *King Gorboduc* a legendary British king who appeared in an early English tragedy

100

Master Parson, am Master Parson; for what is 'that' but 15
that, and 'is' but is?

Toby. To him, Sir Topas.

Clown. What ho, I say. Peace in this prison!

Toby. The knave counterfeits well; a good knave.

Malvolio within.

Malvolio. Who calls there?   20

Clown. Sir Topas the curate, who comes to visit Malvolio
the lunatic.

Malvolio. Sir Topas, Sir Topas, good Sir Topas, go to my
lady.

Clown. Out, hyperbolical fiend! How vexest thou this 25
man! Talkest thou nothing but of ladies?

Toby. Well said, Master Parson.

Malvolio. Sir Topas, never was man thus wronged. Good
Sir Topas, do not think I am mad. They have laid me
here in hideous darkness.   30

Clown. Fie, thou dishonest Satan. I call thee by the most
modest terms, for I am one of those gentle ones that will
use the devil himself with courtesy. Say'st thou that
house is dark?

Malvolio. As hell, Sir Topas.   35

Clown. Why, it hath bay windows transparent as barricadoes, and the clerestories toward the south north are as
lustrous as ebony; and yet complainest thou of obstruction?

Malvolio. I am not mad, Sir Topas. I say to you this house 40
is dark.

Clown. Madman, thou errest. I say there is no darkness but

19 *knave* boy, fellow 25 *hyperbolical* enormous 31 *dishonest* dishonorable
34 *house* darkened room 36-37 *barricadoes* barricades 37 *clerestories*
upper windows

ignorance, in which thou art more puzzled than the
Egyptians in their fog.

45 *Malvolio.* I say this house is as dark as ignorance, though ignorance were as dark as hell; and I say there was never
man thus abused. I am no more mad than you are. Make
the trial of it in any constant question.

Clown. What is the opinion of Pythagoras concerning wild
50 fowl?

Malvolio. That the soul of our grandam might happily in-
habit a bird.

Clown. What think'st thou of his opinion?

Malvolio. I think nobly of the soul and no way approve his
55 opinion.

Clown. Fare thee well. Remain thou still in darkness. Thou
shalt hold th' opinion of Pythagoras ere I will allow of
thy wits, and fear to kill a woodcock, lest thou dispossess
the soul of thy grandam. Fare thee well.

60 *Malvolio.* Sir Topas, Sir Topas!

Toby. My most exquisite Sir Topas!

Clown. Nay, I am for all waters.

Maria. Thou mightst have done this without thy beard and
gown. He sees thee not.

65 *Toby.* To him in thine own voice, and bring me word how
thou find'st him. *[to Maria]* I would we were well rid of
this knavery. If he may be conveniently delivered, I
would he were; for I am now so far in offense with my
niece that I cannot pursue with any safety this sport to the
70 upshot. *[to the Clown]* Come by and by to my chamber.
Exit [with Maria].

44 *fog* (Moses brought a three-day fog on the Egyptians)   48 *constant
question* consistent discussion   49 *Pythagoras* (who originated the doctrine
of transmigration of souls)   51 *happily* haply, by chance   57 *allow of* ac-
knowledge   62 *for all waters* i.e. good for any trade   70 *upshot* outcome

Clown. [sings] 'Hey, Robin, jolly Robin,
                    Tell me how thy lady does.'

Malvolio. Fool.

Clown. 'My lady is unkind, perdie!'

Malvolio. Fool.   75

Clown. 'Alas, why is she so?'

Malvolio. Fool, I say.

Clown. 'She loves another.' Who calls, ha?

Malvolio. Good fool, as ever thou wilt deserve well at my
    hand, help me to a candle, and pen, ink, and paper. As I   80
    am a gentleman, I will live to be thankful to thee for't.

Clown. Master Malvolio?

Malvolio. Ay, good fool.

Clown. Alas, sir, how fell you besides your five wits?

Malvolio. Fool, there was never man so notoriously abused.   85
    I am as well in my wits, fool, as thou art.

Clown. But as well? Then you are mad indeed, if you be
    no better in your wits than a fool.

Malvolio. They have here propertied me; keep me in dark-
    ness, send ministers to me, asses, and do all they can to   90
    face me out of my wits.

Clown. Advise you what you say. The minister is here. —
    Malvolio, Malvolio, thy wits the heavens restore. En-
    deavor thyself to sleep and leave thy vain bibble babble.

Malvolio. Sir Topas.   95

Clown. Maintain no words with him, good fellow. — Who,
    I, sir? Not I, sir. God b' wi' you, good Sir Topas. —
    Marry, amen. — I will, sir, I will.

Malvolio. Fool, fool, fool, I say!

71 *Hey, Robin* ... (from an old song, sometimes attributed to Sir Thomas
Wyatt) 74 *perdie* certainly 84 *besides your five wits* out of your mind
89 *propertied me* made me a property, a mere thing 91 *face me* brazen me
92 *Advise you* be careful

100 *Clown.* Alas, sir, be patient. What say you, sir? I am shent
for speaking to you.

Malvolio. Good fool, help me to some light and some
paper. I tell thee, I am as well in my wits as any man in
Illyria.

105 *Clown.* Well-a-day that you were, sir.

Malvolio. By this hand, I am. Good fool, some ink, paper,
and light; and convey what I will set down to my lady.
It shall advantage thee more than ever the bearing of
letter did.

110 *Clown.* I will help you to't. But tell me true, are you not
mad indeed? or do you but counterfeit?

Malvolio. Believe me, I am not. I tell thee true.

Clown. Nay, I'll ne'er believe a madman till I see his brains.
I will fetch you light and paper and ink.

115 *Malvolio.* Fool, I'll requite it in the highest degree. I prithee
be gone.

Clown. *[sings]*   I am gone, sir,
            And anon, sir,
      I'll be with you again,
120   In a trice,
              Like to the old Vice,
      Your need to sustain.
      Who with dagger of lath,
      In his rage and his wrath,
125   Cries 'Ah ha' to the devil.
      Like a mad lad,
      'Pare thy nails, dad.'
            Adieu, goodman devil.   *Exit.*

100 *shent* reproved 105 *Well-a-day* woe, alas 121 *Vice* comic character
of the morality plays

Enter Sebastian.

Sebastian. This is the air; that is the glorious sun;
   This pearl she gave me, I do feel't and see't;
   And though 'tis wonder that enwraps me thus,
   Yet 'tis not madness. Where's Antonio then?
   I could not find him at the Elephant;   5
   Yet there he was, and there I found this credit,
   That he did range the town to seek me out.
   His counsel now might do me golden service;
   For though my soul disputes well with my sense
   That this may be some error, but no madness,   10
   Yet doth this accident and flood of fortune
   So far exceed all instance, all discourse,
   That I am ready to distrust mine eyes
   And wrangle with my reason that persuades me
   To any other trust but that I am mad,   15
   Or else the lady's mad. Yet, if 'twere so,
   She could not sway her house, command her followers,
   Take and give back affairs and their dispatch
   With such a smooth, discreet, and stable bearing
   As I perceive she does. There's something in't   20
   That is deceivable. But here the lady comes.

Enter Olivia and Priest.

Olivia. Blame not this haste of mine. If you mean well,
   Now go with me and with this holy man
   Into the chantry by. There, before him,
   And underneath that consecrated roof,   25
   Plight me the full assurance of your faith,

IV, iii, 6 *was* had been   *credit* belief   12 *instance* example   *discourse* logic
14 *wrangle* dispute   17 *sway* rule   18 *dispatch* management   21 *deceivable*
deceptive   24 *chantry by* chapel near by

That my most jealous and too doubtful soul
May live at peace. He shall conceal it
Whiles you are willing it shall come to note,
30 What time we will our celebration keep
According to my birth. What do you say?

Sebastian. I'll follow this good man and go with you
And having sworn truth, ever will be true.

Olivia. Then lead the way, good father, and heavens so
shine
35 That they may fairly note this act of mine.   *Exeunt.*

V, i   *Enter Clown and Fabian.*

Fabian. Now as thou lov'st me, let me see his letter.

Clown. Good Master Fabian, grant me another request.

Fabian. Anything.

Clown. Do not desire to see this letter.

5 *Fabian.* This is to give a dog, and in recompense desire my
dog again.

Enter Duke, Viola, Curio, and Lords.

Duke. Belong you to the Lady Olivia, friends?

Clown. Ay, sir, we are some of her trappings.

Duke. I know thee well. How dost thou, my good fellow?

10 *Clown.* Truly, sir, the better for my foes, and the worse for
my friends.

Duke. Just the contrary: the better for thy friends.

Clown. No, sir, the worse.

Duke. How can that be?

15 *Clown.* Marry, sir, they praise me and make an ass of me.

27 *jealous* anxious   29 *Whiles* until

106

Now my foes tell me plainly I am an ass; so that by my
foes, sir, I profit in the knowledge of myself, and by my
friends I am abused; so that, conclusions to be as kisses, if
your four negatives make your two affirmatives, why
then, the worse for my friends, and the better for my foes. 20

Duke. Why, this is excellent.

Clown. By my troth, sir, no, though it please you to be one
of my friends.

Duke. Thou shalt not be the worse for me. There's gold.

Clown. But that it would be double-dealing, sir, I would 25
you could make it another.

Duke. O, you give me ill counsel.

Clown. Put your grace in your pocket, sir, for this once,
and let your flesh and blood obey it.

Duke. Well, I will be so much a sinner to be a double- 30
dealer. There's another.

Clown. Primo, secundo, tertio is a good play; and the old
saying is 'The third pays for all.' The triplex, sir, is a good
tripping measure; or the bells of Saint Bennet, sir, may
put you in mind – one, two, three.   35

Duke. You can fool no more money out of me at this
throw. If you will let your lady know I am here to speak
with her, and bring her along with you, it may awake my
bounty further.

Clown. Marry, sir, lullaby to your bounty till I come again, 40
I go, sir; but I would not have you to think that my
desire of having is the sin of covetousness. But, as you
say, sir, let your bounty take a nap; I will awake it anon.
                                                    Exit.

V, i, 18 *abused* deceived 25 *double-dealing* (1) double giving (2) deceit
28 *your grace* (1) title of address (2) your generosity 32 *play* (probably a
children's game) 33 *triplex* triple time in music 34 *Saint Bennet* St.
Benedict's church 37 *throw* throw of the dice

Enter Antonio and Officers.

Viola. Here comes the man, sir, that did rescue me.
45 *Duke.* That face of his I do remember well;
    Yet when I saw it last, it was besmeared
    As black as Vulcan in the smoke of war.
    A baubling vessel was he captain of,
    For shallow draught and bulk unprizable,
50   With which such scathful grapple did he make
    With the most noble bottom of our fleet
    That very envy and the tongue of loss
    Cried fame and honor on him. What's the matter?
1. Officer. Orsino, this is that Antonio
55   That took the Phoenix and her fraught from Candy;
    And this is he that did the Tiger board
    When your young nephew Titus lost his leg.
    Here in the streets, desperate of shame and state,
    In private brabble did we apprehend him.
60 *Viola.* He did me kindness, sir; drew on my side;
    But in conclusion put strange speech upon me.
    I know not what 'twas but distraction.
Duke. Notable pirate, thou salt-water thief,
    What foolish boldness brought thee to their mercies
65   Whom thou in terms so bloody and so dear
    Hast made thine enemies?
Antonio.   Orsino, noble sir,
    Be pleased that I shake off these names you give me.
    Antonio never yet was thief or pirate,
    Though I confess, on base and ground enough,

---

47 *Vulcan* Roman god of fire and patron of metal workers 48 *baubling*
trifling 49 *unprizable* unworthy of being taken as a prize 50 *scathful*
harmful 51 *bottom* ship 52 *very envy* even malice *loss* the losers 55
fraught cargo *Candy* Candia, Crete 58 *desperate* reckless 59 *brabble*
brawl 62 *distraction* madness 65 *dear* costly 69 *base and ground* solid
grounds

Orsino's enemy. A witchcraft drew me hither.   70
That most ingrateful boy there by your side
From the rude sea's enraged and foamy mouth
Did I redeem. A wrack past hope he was.
His life I gave him, and did thereto add
My love without retention or restraint,   75
All his in dedication. For his sake
Did I expose myself (pure for his love)
Into the danger of this adverse town;
Drew to defend him when he was beset;
Where being apprehended, his false cunning   80
(Not meaning to partake with me in danger)
Taught him to face me out of his acquaintance,
And grew a twenty years removèd thing
While one would wink; denied me mine own purse,
Which I had recommended to his use   85
Not half an hour before.
Viola.   How can this be?
Duke. When came he to this town?
Antonio. To-day, my lord; and for three months before,
No int'rim, not a minute's vacancy,
Both day and night did we keep company.   90

Enter Olivia and Attendants.

Duke. Here comes the Countess; now heaven walks on
    earth.
But for thee, fellow: fellow, thy words are madness.
Three months this youth hath tended upon me;
But more of that anon. Take him aside.
Olivia. What would my lord, but that he may not
    have,   95

77 *pure* purely 82 *face . . . acquaintance* pretend not to know me 83 *re-*
movèd estranged 85 *recommended* entrusted 95 *but that* except what

109

    Wherein Olivia may seem serviceable?
    Cesario, you do not keep promise with me.
Viola. Madam?
Duke. Gracious Olivia —
100 *Olivia.* What do you say, Cesario? — Good my lord —
    Viola. My lord would speak; my duty hushes me.
    Olivia. If it be aught to the old tune, my lord,
      It is as fat and fulsome to mine ear
      As howling after music.
    Duke.   Still so cruel?
105 *Olivia.* Still so constant, lord.
    Duke. What, to perverseness? You uncivil lady,
      To whose ingrate and unauspicious altars
      My soul the faithfull'st off'rings hath breathed out
      That e'er devotion tendered. What shall I do?
110 *Olivia.* Even what it please my lord, that shall become him.
    Duke. Why should I not, had I the heart to do it,
      Like to th' Egyptian thief at point of death,
      Kill what I love? (A savage jealousy
      That sometime savors nobly.) But hear me this:
115   Since you to non-regardance cast my faith,
      And that I partly know the instrument
      That screws me from my true place in your favor,
      Live you the marble-breasted tyrant still.
      But this your minion, whom I know you love,
120   And whom, by heaven I swear, I tender dearly,
      Him will I tear out of that cruel eye
      Where he sits crownèd in his master's spite.
      Come, boy, with me. My thoughts are ripe in mischief.

---

103 *fat* superfluous *fulsome* offensive 112 *th' Egyptian thief* Thyamis in
the *Aethiopica* by Heliodorus 115 *non-regardance* neglect 117 *screws* pries
119 *minion* favorite 120 *tender* hold 122 *in . . . spite* despite his master

I'll sacrifice the lamb that I do love
To spite a raven's heart within a dove.   *[Going.]* 125
Viola. And I, most jocund, apt, and willingly,
To do you rest a thousand deaths would die. *[Following.]*
Olivia. Where goes Cesario?
Viola.   After him I love
More than I love these eyes, more than my life,
More, by all mores, than e'er I shall love wife.   130
If I do feign, you witnesses above
Punish my life for tainting of my love!
Olivia. Ay me detested! how am I beguiled!
Viola. Who does beguile you? Who does do you wrong?
Olivia. Hast thou forgot thyself? Is it so long?   135
Call forth the holy father.   *[Exit an Attendant.]*
Duke.   *[to Viola]* Come, away!
Olivia. Whither, my lord? Cesario, husband, stay.
Duke. Husband?
Olivia.   Ay, husband. Can he that deny?
Duke. Her husband, sirrah?
Viola.   No, my lord, not I.
Olivia. Alas, it is the baseness of thy fear   140
That makes thee strangle thy propriety.
Fear not, Cesario; take thy fortunes up;
Be that thou know'st thou art, and then thou art
As great as that thou fear'st.

Enter Priest.

                         O, welcome, father!
Father, I charge thee by thy reverence   145

126 *apt* properly 127 *do you rest* give you peace 130 *all mores* i.e. all
conceivable comparisons 141 *propriety* identity 144 *that thou fear'st* i.e.
the Duke

III

Here to unfold — though lately we intended
To keep in darkness what occasion now
Reveals before 'tis ripe — what thou dost know
Hath newly passed between this youth and me.

150 *Priest.* A contract of eternal bond of love,
Confirmed by mutual joinder of your hands,
Attested by the holy close of lips,
Strength'ned by interchangement of your rings;
And all the ceremony of this compact

155 Sealed in my function, by my testimony;
Since when, my watch hath told me, toward my grave
I have travelled but two hours.

Duke. O thou dissembling cub, what wilt thou be
When time hath sowed a grizzle on thy case?

160 Or will not else thy craft so quickly grow
That thine own trip shall be thine overthrow?
Farewell, and take her; but direct thy feet
Where thou and I, henceforth, may never meet.

Viola. My lord, I do protest.

Olivia.   O, do not swear.

165 Hold little faith, though thou hast too much fear.

Enter Sir Andrew.

Andrew. For the love of God, a surgeon! Send one presently to Sir Toby.

Olivia. What's the matter?

Andrew. Has broke my head across, and has given Sir

170 Toby a bloody coxcomb too. For the love of God, your
help! I had rather than forty pound I were at home.

Olivia. Who has done this, Sir Andrew?

---

152 *close* meeting   159 *a grizzle* grey hair   *case* sheath, i.e. skin   161 *trip*
trickery   165 *little* a little   166–67 *presently* at once   169 *Has* he has

Andrew. The Count's gentleman, one Cesario. We took
him for a coward, but he's the very devil incardinate.

Duke. My gentleman Cesario?   175

Andrew. Od's lifelings, here he is! You broke my head for
nothing; and that that I did, I was set on to do't by Sir
Toby.

Viola. Why do you speak to me? I never hurt you.
You drew your sword upon me without cause,   180
But I bespake you fair and hurt you not.

Enter [Sir] Toby and Clown.

Andrew. If a bloody coxcomb be a hurt, you have hurt me.
I think you set nothing by a bloody coxcomb. Here
comes Sir Toby halting; you shall hear more. But if he
had not been in drink, he would have tickled you other-   185
gates than he did.

Duke. How now, gentleman? How is't with you?

Toby. That's all one! Has hurt me, and there's th' end on't.
Sot, didst see Dick Surgeon, sot?

Clown. O, he's drunk, Sir Toby, an hour agone. His eyes   190
were set at eight i' th' morning.

Toby. Then he's a rogue and a passy measures pavin. I hate
a drunken rogue.

Olivia. Away with him! Who hath made this havoc with
them?   195

Andrew. I'll help you, Sir Toby, because we'll be dressed together.

Toby. Will you help? An ass-head and a coxcomb and a
knave, a thin-faced knave, a gull?

---

174 *incardinate* incarnate   184 *halting* limping   185–86 *othergates* otherwise
191 *set* fixed or gone down, i.e. closed   192 *passy measures pavin* an eight-
bar double-slow dance

200 *Olivia.* Get him to bed, and let his hurt be looked to.
    [Exeunt Clown, Fabian, Sir Toby, and Sir Andrew.]

Enter Sebastian.

Sebastian. I am sorry, madam, I have hurt your kinsman;
  But had it been the brother of my blood,
  I must have done no less with wit and safety.
  You throw a strange regard upon me, and by that
205 I do perceive it hath offended you.
  Pardon me, sweet one, even for the vows
  We made each other but so late ago.
Duke. One face, one voice, one habit, and two persons —
  A natural perspective that is and is not.
210 *Sebastian.* Antonio, O my dear Antonio,
  How have the hours racked and tortured me
  Since I have lost thee!
Antonio. Sebastian are you?
Sebastian.   Fear'st thou that, Antonio?
Antonio. How have you made division of yourself?
215 An apple cleft in two is not more twin
  Than these two creatures. Which is Sebastian?
Olivia. Most wonderful.
Sebastian. Do I stand there? I never had a brother;
  Nor can there be that deity in my nature
220 Of here and everywhere. I had a sister,
  Whom the blind waves and surges have devoured.
  Of charity, what kin are you to me?
  What countryman? What name? What parentage?
Viola. Of Messaline; Sebastian was my father;
225 Such a Sebastian was my brother too;

---

203 *wit and safety* intelligent regard for my safety   204 *strange regard* estranged look   208 *habit* dress   209 *perspective* glass producing an optical illusion

So went he suited to his watery tomb.
If spirits can assume both form and suit,
You come to fright us.
Sebastian.   A spirit I am indeed,
 But am in that dimension grossly clad
 Which from the womb I did participate.   230
 Were you a woman, as the rest goes even,
 I should my tears let fall upon your cheek
 And say, 'Thrice welcome, drownèd Viola!'
Viola. My father had a mole upon his brow.
Sebastian. And so had mine.   235
Viola. And died that day when Viola from her birth
 Had numb'red thirteen years.
Sebastian. O, that record is lively in my soul!
 He finishèd indeed his mortal act
 That day that made my sister thirteen years.   240
Viola. If nothing lets to make us happy both
 But this my masculine usurped attire,
 Do not embrace me till each circumstance
 Of place, time, fortune do cohere and jump
 That I am Viola; which to confirm,   245
 I'll bring you to a captain in this town,
 Where lie my maiden weeds; by whose gentle help
 I was preserved to serve this noble Count.
 All the occurrence of my fortune since
 Hath been between this lady and this lord.   250
Sebastian. [to Olivia] So comes it, lady, you have been mis-
  took.
 But nature to her bias drew in that.

226 *suited* dressed 229 *dimension* form *grossly* in the flesh 230 *participate*
inherit 231 *rest goes even* other circumstances allow 238 *record* memory
241 *lets* hinders 244 *jump* agree completely 247 *weeds* clothes 252 *to
her bias drew* i.e. drew you into a natural course

You would have been contracted to a maid;
Nor are you therein, by my life, deceived:
255   You are betrothed both to a maid and man.
Duke. Be not amazed; right noble is his blood.
If this be so, as yet the glass seems true,
I shall have share in this most happy wrack.
[To Viola] Boy, thou hast said to me a thousand times
260   Thou never shouldst love woman like to me.
Viola. And all those sayings will I over swear,
And all those swearings keep as true in soul
As doth that orbèd continent the fire
That severs day from night.
Duke.   Give me thy hand,
265   And let me see thee in thy woman's weeds.
Viola. The captain that did bring me first on shore
Hath my maid's garments. He upon some action
Is now in durance, at Malvolio's suit,
A gentleman, and follower of my lady's.
270 *Olivia.* He shall enlarge him. Fetch Malvolio hither.
And yet alas, now I remember me,
They say, poor gentleman, he's much distract.

Enter Clown with a letter, and Fabian.

A most extracting frenzy of mine own
From my remembrance clearly banished his.
275   How does he, sirrah?
Clown. Truly, madam, he holds Belzebub at the stave's end
as well as a man in his case may do. Has here writ a letter
to you; I should have given't you to-day morning. But

---

257 *glass* perspective glass   261 *over swear* swear over again   263 *orbèd*
continent sphere of the sun   267 *action* legal charge   270 *enlarge* free   273
extracting distracting   276 *holds . . . end* i.e. holds the devil off

as a madman's epistles are no gospels, so it skills not much
when they are delivered.   280

Olivia. Open't and read it.

Clown. Look then to be well edified, when the fool delivers
the madman. *[Reads in a loud voice]* 'By the Lord,
madam' —

Olivia. How now? Art thou mad?   285

Clown. No, madam, I do but read madness. An your ladyship will have it as it ought to be, you must allow vox.

Olivia. Prithee read i' thy right wits.

Clown. So I do, madonna; but to read his right wits is to
read thus. Therefore perpend, my princess, and give ear. 290

Olivia. *[to Fabian]* Read it you, sirrah.

Fabian. *(reads)* 'By the Lord, madam, you wrong me, and
the world shall know it. Though you have put me into
darkness, and given your drunken cousin rule over me,
yet have I the benefit of my senses as well as your lady- 295
ship. I have your own letter that induced me to the sem-
blance I put on; with the which I doubt not but to do
myself much right, or you much shame. Think of me as
you please. I leave my duty a little unthought of, and
speak out of my injury.   300
                    'THE MADLY USED MALVOLIO.'

Olivia. Did he write this?

Clown. Ay, madam.

Duke. This savors not much of distraction.

Olivia. See him delivered, Fabian; bring him hither.   305
                                        [Exit Fabian.]
My lord, so please you, these things further thought on,
To think me as well a sister as a wife,

279 *skills* matters 282 *delivers* speaks the words of 287 *vox* voice-volume
290 *perpend* consider

One day shall crown th' alliance on't, so please you,
Here at my house and at my proper cost.
310 *Duke.* Madam, I am most apt t' embrace your offer.
    [*To Viola*] Your master quits you; and for your service
        done him,
    So much against the mettle of your sex,
    So far beneath your soft and tender breeding,
    And since you called me master for so long,
315 Here is my hand; you shall from this time be
    Your master's mistress.
Olivia.   A sister; you are she.

        Enter [Fabian, with] Malvolio.

Duke. Is this the madman?
Olivia.   Ay, my lord, this same.
    How now, Malvolio?
Malvolio.   Madam, you have done me wrong,
    Notorious wrong.
Olivia.   Have I, Malvolio? No.
320 *Malvolio.* Lady, you have. Pray you peruse that letter.
    You must not now deny it is your hand.
    Write from it if you can, in hand or phrase,
    Or say 'tis not your seal, not your invention.
    You can say none of this. Well, grant it then,
325 And tell me, in the modesty of honor,
    Why you have given me such clear lights of favor,
    Bade me come smiling and cross-gartered to you,
    To put on yellow stockings, and to frown
    Upon Sir Toby and the lighter people;
330 And, acting this in an obedient hope,

309 *proper* own 310 *apt* ready 311 *quits* releases 322 *from it* differently
323 *invention* composition 325 *in . . . honor* with honorable propriety
329 *lighter* lesser

Why have you suffered me to be imprisoned,
Kept in a dark house, visited by the priest,
And made the most notorious geck and gull
That e'er invention played on? Tell me why.

Olivia. Alas, Malvolio, this is not my writing,   335
Though I confess much like the character;
But, out of question, 'tis Maria's hand.
And now I do bethink me, it was she
First told me thou wast mad. Thou cam'st in smiling,
And in such forms which here were presupposed   340
Upon thee in the letter. Prithee be content.
This practice hath most shrewdly passed upon thee;
But when we know the grounds and authors of it,
Thou shalt be both the plaintiff and the judge
Of thine own cause.

Fabian.   Good madam, hear me speak,   345
And let no quarrel, nor no brawl to come,
Taint the condition of this present hour,
Which I have wond'red at. In hope it shall not,
Most freely I confess myself and Toby
Set this device against Malvolio here,   350
Upon some stubborn and uncourteous parts
We had conceived against him. Maria writ
The letter, at Sir Toby's great importance,
In recompense whereof he hath married her.
How with a sportful malice it was followed   355
May rather pluck on laughter than revenge,
If that the injuries be justly weighed
That have on both sides passed.

Olivia. Alas, poor fool, how have they baffled thee!

333 *geck and gull* ludicrous dupe   340-41 *presupposed Upon thee* put upon
you beforehand   342 *shrewdly passed* maliciously been put   351 *Upon* on
account of   353 *importance* importunity   359 *baffled thee* disgraced you
publicly

360 Clown. Why, 'some are born great, some achieve greatness,
     and some have greatness thrown upon them.' I was one,
     sir, in this interlude, one Sir Topas, sir; but that's all one.
     'By the Lord, fool, I am not mad!' But do you remem-
     ber, 'Madam, why laugh you at such a barren rascal?
365 An you smile not, he's gagged'? And thus the whirligig
     of time brings in his revenges.
     Malvolio. I'll be revenged on the whole pack of you!
                                                    [Exit.]

     Olivia. He hath been most notoriously abused.
     Duke. Pursue him and entreat him to a peace.
370 He hath not told us of the captain yet.
     When that is known, and golden time convents,
     A solemn combination shall be made
     Of our dear souls. Meantime, sweet sister,
     We will not part from hence. Cesario, come —
375 For so you shall be while you are a man,
     But when in other habits you are seen,
     Orsino's mistress and his fancy's queen.
                              Exeunt [all but the Clown].

                    Clown sings.

     When that I was and a little tiny boy,
         With hey, ho, the wind and the rain,
380 A foolish thing was but a toy,
         For the rain it raineth every day.

     But when I came to man's estate,
         With hey, ho, the wind and the rain,
     'Gainst knaves and thieves men shut their gate,
385   For the rain it raineth every day.

---

362 interlude an early form of dramatic entertainment 371 convents is
convenient 377 fancy's love's

But when I came, alas, to wive,
  With hey, ho, the wind and the rain,
By swaggering could I never thrive,
  For the rain it raineth every day.

But when I came unto my beds,   390
  With hey, ho, the wind and the rain,
With tosspots still had drunken heads,
  For the rain it raineth every day.

A great while ago the world begun,
  With hey, ho, the wind and the rain;   395
But that's all one, our play is done,
  And we'll strive to please you every day.

                                    [Exit.]

Details of the
Pelican Shakespeare and
other Penguin series
follow.

THE PELICAN SHAKESPEARE

General Editor: Alfred Harbage

Tragedies

Edited by Maynard Mack	ANTONY AND CLEOPATRA
Harry Levin	CORIOLANUS
Willard Farnham	HAMLET
S. F. Johnson	JULIUS CAESAR
Alfred Harbage	KING LEAR
Alfred Harbage	MACBETH
Gerald E. Bentley	OTHELLO
John E. Hankins	ROMEO AND JULIET
Charlton Hinman	TIMON OF ATHENS
Gustav Cross	TITUS ANDRONICUS

Comedies

Jonas Barish	ALL'S WELL THAT ENDS WELL
Ralph Sargent	AS YOU LIKE IT
Paul A. Jorgensen	THE COMEDY OF ERRORS
Robert B. Heilman	CYMBELINE
Alfred Harbage	LOVE'S LABOR'S LOST
R. C. Bald	MEASURE FOR MEASURE
Brents Stirling	THE MERCHANT OF VENICE
Fredson T. Bowers	THE MERRY WIVES OF WINDSOR
Madeleine Doran	A MIDSUMMER NIGHT'S DREAM
Josephine Waters Bennett	MUCH ADO ABOUT NOTHING
James McManaway	PERICLES
Richard Hosley	THE TAMING OF THE SHREW
Northrop Frye	THE TEMPEST
Virgil Whitaker	TROILUS AND CRESSIDA
Charles Prouty	TWELFTH NIGHT
Berners Jackson	TWO GENTLEMEN OF VERONA
Baldwin Maxwell	THE WINTER'S TALE

Histories and Poems

M. A. Shaaber	HENRY IV, PART I
Allan Chester	HENRY IV, PART II
Alfred Harbage	HENRY V
David Bevington	HENRY VI, PART I
George Williams	HENRY VI, PART II
Robert K. Turner, Jr.	HENRY VI, PART III
F. D. Hoeniger	HENRY VIII
Irving Ribner	KING JOHN
Matthew Black	RICHARD II
G. Blakemore Evans	RICHARD III
Richard Wilbur	THE POEMS
Douglas Bush	THE SONNETS

PLAYS BY BERNARD SHAW

*The following plays are published
in Penguin editions. Each play has the
complete text and the
author's preface.*

ANDROCLES AND THE LION

THE APPLE CART

ARMS AND THE MAN

BACK TO METHUSELAH

CAESAR AND CLEOPATRA

CANDIDA

THE DEVIL'S DISCIPLE

THE DOCTOR'S DILEMMA

HEARTBREAK HOUSE

MAJOR BARBARA

MAN AND SUPERMAN

THE MILLIONAIRESS

PLAYS UNPLEASANT

PYGMALION

SAINT JOAN

SELECTED ONE-ACT PLAYS

SEVEN ONE-ACT PLAYS

THREE SOVIET PLAYS

CHAUCER: THE CANTERBURY TALES

A Modern Version By
Nevill Coghill

This is the first English work to be included in the Penguin Classics series of modern translations. When it was published it was widely acclaimed as a means of bringing Chaucer to thousands of people who would never have read him otherwise. Reviewers were quick to realize that Mr Coghill, who is a fellow of Exeter College, Oxford, was the right person to have attempted the task.

Punch offered very high praise by saying '... this translation will remain a beloved classic until the language changes again sufficiently to call for another renaissance'. *The Manchester Guardian* found that 'Mr Coghill has achieved his aim that his translation should be considered as a poem and not as a crib'. And the most enthusiastic welcome came from *The Times Educational Supplement* which said, 'Altogether Mr Coghill's achievement is remarkable. He has been almost consistently successful and his practice carries out his theory and intentions. The bland, humorous, observing, and courtly spirit that informs the original is somehow preserved in a different idiom'.